Buckinghamshire Stories of the Supernatural

David Kidd-Hewitt

COUNTRYSIDE BOOKS

NEWBURY, BERKSHIRE

First published 2008
© David Kidd-Hewitt, 2008

COUNTRYSIDE BOOKS
3 Catherine Road
Newbury, Berkshire

To view our complete range of books,
please visit us at
www.countrysidebooks.co.uk

ISBN 978 1 84674 118 0

For Jack Ethan Garland
with much love
from his grandpa

Cover picture courtesy of the Hell-Fire Caves, West Wycombe

Designed by Peter Davies, Nautilus Design
Produced through MRM Associates Ltd., Reading
Typeset by Jean Cussons Typesetting, Diss, Norfolk
Printed by Information Press, Oxford

All material for the manufacture
of this book was sourced from
sustainable forests

Contents

Acknowledgements

So many people have been generous with their time, their stories and their honesty in relating their supernatural experiences to me. It is a shock, and a never-to-be-forgotten experience, when the supernatural touches your life and I found that all those who assisted me in making this book were still seeking more worldly, everyday explanations for what occurred. Indeed, I have done the same, but up to now have failed.

We all, therefore, offer you a collection of supernatural stories of Buckinghamshire spanning time up to the present day. It is easy to spot where a 'pinch of salt' may be required for my occasional dip into a legend or two, but my contributors' stories require no such superstitious ritual. They truly experienced the supernatural. They are David, Leslee, Georgina (and Rio); James; Roy; Bob and Tom; Sharon; Owen, Damon and Sandra; Richard and Natalie; Julie, Jimmy and Claire; Linda; Barbara and Kirsty; David and Stephen; Beryl and Jean; Bob; Diana; Mark and Allyson; John from Chesham; Violet and John; Audrey and Jane; Norma and Bernard; Margery; and Katie.

I am grateful also to those who assisted me by allowing me privileged access to private locations as well as to their own researched stories, files and contacts – Vivienne Rae-Ellis, author; Roy Hickman, director of Woodrow High House; Sqn. Ldr. Colin Baker, Communications Officer, RAF Halton; Diana Canning, legal expert witness; John Pilgrim, broadcaster and writer; Revd David Horner; Sharon Neill, medium; Bob Eastland of the Swan Theatre security; Tom Schoon, Swan Theatre press officer; Damon Torsten and Owen Pellow, crcmh website; Simon Cornwell, urban explorer; Sarah Jane and Gill of Soulseekers; Jason Hawes and Grant Wilson of The Atlantic Paranormal Society (TAPS); Betty Puttick, author; Hell-Fire Caves staff; Lewis Kitchener, author; Richard Barber, journalist; Bob Pugsley, landlord, the Chequers; Audrey Barrett, manager, the Ivy House; Katharine Matthews, Dundridge Manor; Jo McParlane with Violet and John Cowley at Hamilton House; John Vince, Ellesborough historian; Jenny Howe, Mayor's Parlour, High Wycombe.

Additional thanks for research assistance to Linda Tucker and Penny Pettitt at Great Missenden Library; Sally Price, Sarah Hambling and Kim Farrell at Marlow Tourist Information, Roger Bettridge, County Archivist; The Horace Harman estate for extracts from Buckinghamshire Dialect (Hazell, Watson & Viney Ltd, Aylesbury 1929.

Map of Buckinghamshire

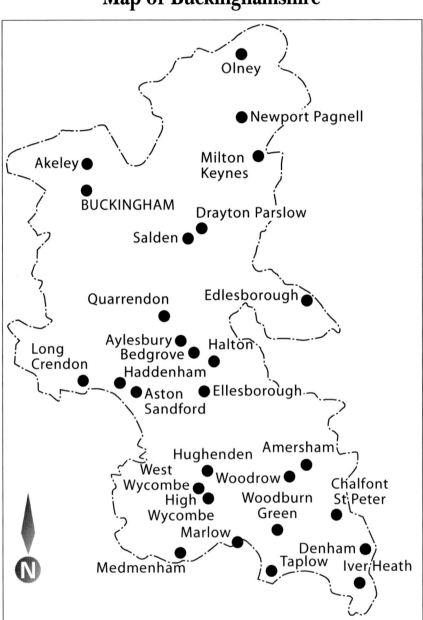

Olney

Newport Pagnell

Akeley

Milton Keynes

BUCKINGHAM

Drayton Parslow

Salden

Quarrendon

Edlesborough

Aylesbury
Bedgrove
Haddenham

Halton

Long Crendon

Aston Sandford

Ellesborough

Hughenden

Amersham

West Wycombe

Woodrow

High Wycombe

Woodburn Green

Chalfont St Peter

Marlow

Medmenham

Denham

Taplow

Iver Heath

N

Introduction

IN our fast-moving, 21st-century world, where science and technology dominate our everyday lives, a growing interest in the supernatural would seem to be a contradiction. Yet, perhaps it isn't. We live with facts, figures and scientific knowledge on the one hand, and the unexplained mysterious world of spirits and hauntings on the other, and many of us seem to be able and willing to absorb both into our lives.

Modern technology in the form of night-vision digital cameras, motion sensors, sophisticated temperature measuring devices and electronic voice phenomena (EVP) recorders is the most basic equipment used by investigators of the paranormal. Attempts to find evidence of supernatural activity have become popular home entertainment, with television programmes such as *Most Haunted* tempting us into the world of the unexplained. Websites devoted to both supernatural and paranormal investigations have proliferated since the millennium.

The supernatural is commonly defined as 'events that have no natural explanation'. Entities, forces or phenomena which defy and go beyond natural laws. Paranormal is used as a catch-all term to include the supernatural and much more besides – for example, UFOs, the Bermuda Triangle, crop circles, and claimed personal attributes such as telepathy and extra-sensory perception.

When I wrote *Buckinghamshire Tales of Mystery and Murder* in 2003, there were only a handful of websites dedicated to locating and investigating paranormal activities or recounting tales of ghostly happenings – now I would be hardpressed to count them, they are multiplying so rapidly. Apart from many more people setting themselves up as ghost or paranormal investigators in the UK and even worldwide, more and more local, county-based groups are forming.

They are devising intricate websites with discussion forums, social events and plans for paranormal expeditions. It has become a very sociable activity – the ultimate 21st-century hobby combining friendship and outings with being pleasurably scared in the dark – but not alone – and you can laugh about it in the pub later. You can play with all kinds of electronic gizmos, set up experiments, learn a bit of history (essential if you want to catalogue your ghosts), and plot all the adventures onto an internet map with the enthusiasm of a stamp collector hinging in a rare stamp.

Internet browsers can then chance across your map, click on a place-name and read the ghostly tales therein. The more adventurous groups also add UFO sightings to their repertoire.

But here is the rub. The reports, tales and stories tend to be scant. 'The devil is in the detail' runs the saying but more often than not you would find it difficult to locate very much ghostly detail let alone a devil.

Wherever possible, *Buckinghamshire Stories of the Supernatural* has tried to use first-hand accounts of all the stories told here and as much background evidence has been hunted down as possible to authenticate the tale. 'A pinch of salt' may remain but quickly throw it over your left shoulder, delve into Buckinghamshire's supernatural stories and, dear reader, repeat after me:

From ghoulies and ghosties
and long-leggedy beasties
and things that go bump in the night,
Good Lord, deliver us!
(Anon)

David Kidd-Hewitt

1

Conversations (and a Cuddle) with a Ghost in Marlow

'I<small>T</small> was pitch black. I woke up feeling a cold breeze on my face and I was really thirsty. Mum and dad were fast asleep so I quietly went downstairs, got my drink but the cold breeze was worse. It was then I noticed that the back door was wide open and I could hear distant barking.

'I went out and I saw Rio barking at something and there was a figure in the back of the garden – a man – and next to him was a dog scratching at the gate. I was so scared. Rio didn't go towards them, which was strange, and he suddenly stopped barking and ran inside to his bed whimpering. I sort of looked at the man – he was just standing there – I blinked again – he was still there, very tall.

'I saw this little dog – he was white, just white. I ran inside and locked the door. I didn't wake mum and dad. They were cross when I told them in the morning, but I felt the house was okay and I had Rio with me.'

Georgina was 13 years old in November 2007 at the time of her scary encounter with the tall man and his dog in the garden. She did not know that mum, Leslee, and dad, David, had already experienced unexplained events only months earlier and were now convinced that the family home they had moved into in the summer of 2006, in Marlow, was haunted.

Leslee told me, 'It still happens now, lock the back door and in the morning it's open. It's quite freaky.' Rio, as we shall learn, would have a lot to tell if only he had a way.

Their story begins at the end of August 2007 when Leslee's older daughter Layla and boyfriend were visiting for a summer barbecue and drinks in the garden. Leslee and Layla do not see each other as often as they would like, so they really make the most of the times they are together and this was no exception.

It was already late, close to midnight or thereabouts, and so David starting to feel chilly, had lit the patio heater. Leslee began thinking about her mother, and she told Layla, and her boyfriend John, of a conversation they had once had about death and dying and confided that her mum had promised her she would try and contact her when the inevitable happened. Leslee suddenly suggested they held a séance to try and talk to mum. David wasn't too happy, but Leslee said it wasn't going to hurt anybody, so they lit lots of candles, held hands and tried to make contact.

John and David didn't take it too seriously and were making fun; they'd had a few whiskies and Leslee told them it wasn't going to work if they didn't take it seriously.

'Anyway we carried on,' recounted Leslee, 'and we tried to call up my mother. She had always said to me she would come back if she could. I said, "Come on, you said you'd come back. Please show me that you can come back." Nothing happened, we waited and waited and nothing happened.'

After 20 minutes, maybe half an hour, the séance was abandoned and they started to drift inside to bed.

About one week later, again quite late, Leslee and David were sitting in the kitchen at their breakfast bar having a chat before going to bed. Suddenly Leslee had said, 'Sssshh – I can hear something!'

David listened, and agreed, he could hear something too. It was a kind of distant thumping noise. Leslee thought it might be next door's rabbit out in his garden hutch. Its name was actually Thumper and it could make quite a loud noise. Too loud for a rabbit, David thought. It wasn't clear where the noise was coming from – it was just in the air, in the distance, yet it was in the kitchen.

Leslee said, 'You're not knocking are you?'

'Course not, you can see I'm not,' retorted David.

Leslee told me, 'So we sat there and I started knocking back – so when it knocked twice, or three times – I did twice or three times back. Then I started doing four, and then it matched what I was doing, so if I did six, it would do six, I did two, it did two. David said to me, "I don't like this."

'I thought this is fascinating, so I said, "I'll do it one more time if you don't believe me David."

'David said, "Well, I'm here, I'm listening to it," then he suggested "Do ten!" So I went thump, thump … to ten – waited for a bit – and I heard this ten back. David said, "There's definitely something trying to talk to you." '

Leslee decided to find out, but first David quickly went upstairs to check on Georgina to make sure she wasn't playing around – she was fast asleep. Back down in the kitchen, Leslee had decided to ask questions and use one knock for 'yes' and two knocks for 'no'.

'Mum is that you?' Two knocks immediately followed Leslee's question.

'So it's not your mum,' said David. 'Hang on a minute, this isn't right – it's really weird.'

Leslee persevered, 'Is there somebody here?' One knock was the reply. Leslee and David continued with the questions and over the next hour and half began to accept that a supernatural force was in communication with them. It was a man who used to live there although the house only dates from the 1970s. He had been living on that site but they failed to establish a date.

'By going through people's names,' David told me, 'we learnt he was called Paul, that he lived here and he died before he should have done. He wasn't murdered, it seemed to be as a result of an accident. He had a family, he had a dog. They are all dead.'

As the questions continued, Rio suddenly got up from his bed and sat transfixed – staring. Leslee said, 'Where are you?' then, realising Paul couldn't answer that question, she quickly added, 'Are you in the kitchen?' No answer at all. 'Are you near our dog?'

One knock followed. Rio was very nervous and shifted uneasily, staring at something unseen close to David and Leslee.

Then it all finished – the communication was broken, Rio went back to his bed and David and Leslee were left with all kinds of thoughts whirling around in their minds. A conversation with a ghost is quite an experience to mull over. One thing was certain, they agreed not to tell 13-year-old Georgina of their experience.

However, during the week that followed, they had endless trouble with Rio. He had been trained as a puppy not to go upstairs. His territory was down in the hall and the kitchen area but over the week that followed the communication with Paul, he kept running upstairs at night and moving around the bathroom. Leslee told me, 'The dog was driving us nuts because he kept coming upstairs. I could hear him pattering around and going in the bathroom like he was scared of something to the point where I'm putting stuff at the top of the stairs to block it, but he wouldn't stay downstairs.'

Rio, it should be revealed, is no puny little dog but a Bull Mastiff/ Great Dane cross – a hunting breed of great renown, tall, heavy and, it seems, scared of ghosts.

David added, 'It would be a real struggle to get him back downstairs again, he weighs ten stone and he fought to go back up as I was dragging him down.'

After a week of this, David and Leslee heard the tapping again when they were in the kitchen. They had not dared start it again but they did not have to. Georgina was safely in bed so Leslee decided to carry on with the bizarre experience.

'Is that Paul?' she asked.

One knock followed.

'Do you like dogs?'

One knock.

'Do you like Rio?'

One knock.

'Did you have a dog of your own?'

Yes, one knock.

'Do you go and see Rio?'

One knock.

'You are scaring him,' said Leslee, 'and he's coming upstairs. Will you stop doing that? Please leave him alone!'

One knock confirmed a yes.

David told me, 'It is such a bizarre conversation, especially when you start repeating it – it's stupid. The conversation went on but we couldn't really find out very much more this time. I remember Leslee said "Do you mean us any harm?" and he said he didn't. She asked him if he ever went upstairs and he said no. We guessed that there were no stairs in his time to climb, it was all at ground level and around the area of the kitchen extension.'

Rio was now content to stay downstairs, only fleeing back up again on understandable occasions such as firework night. Paul, it seemed, had kept to his word – or knock.

Leslee had confided in her daughter Layla who just thought her mum was crazy, but this was soon to change. Layla visited for the weekend, and it was going to be a late night of catching up and having a good time together. However, Leslee wanted to see if Paul was around to prove to Layla that it was true. So she began to knock, asking for Paul. Nothing happened and Layla accused them of having a joke with her. Then the tapping started. Leslee nudged Layla and asked her if she had heard it. At first she didn't and then when she did, she accused David of doing it with his feet. So David moved to another room.

As Leslee began the one-knock-two-knock conversation, Layla accused David of banging on the wall, so he came back in the kitchen and stood clearly visible with his arms folded until Layla was satisfied it couldn't be him.

'Are you near us?' asked Layla.

One knock confirmed yes.

'Are you in the corner of the kitchen – tell us where you are?'

This wasn't a question Paul could answer but suddenly David felt absolutely frozen – the temperature plummeted. David had had enough and left to sit in the other room.

'Are you by the oven?'

Two knocks – no.

'Are you by the bin?'

No, again.

Then Leslee looked directly at Layla, they were sitting one seat apart at the breakfast counter ever since David had left the room. They both knew what the next question had to be.

'Are you in between us?'

A measured pause followed – then one knock.

Leslee told me, 'I'm going cold now just thinking about it.'

Remarkably, Layla asked a totally unexpected question 'Would you like a cuddle Paul?'

A single knock followed and Layla reached over and cuddled the empty air between them. Then it was over.

After Georgina had her November night-time adventure, mum and dad decided they could tell her what had been going on and that possibly she has been the only one to glimpse Paul and his dog outside in the garden.

Nothing much has been heard from Paul this year. 'I know when he's here. I feel this kind of presence.' Leslee told me. Lately, however, David and Leslee have become a little exasperated by lots of small incidents like missing car keys, mobile phones and a digital camera, cracked drinking glasses, CDs laid out in patterns on the floor.

'You've got to go, you're annoying me now,' was Leslee's last request. Leslee and David have decided, for the time being, that their conversations with a ghost should be laid to rest.

Postscript – Summer 2008

Whilst digging at the bottom of David and Leslee's garden to build a summer house, contractors unearthed the bones of a small dog.

2

Sinister Forces: The Haunted Taplow Hospital

'CLIVEDEN VILLAGE is a new-age exclusive development … on the grounds of the former Canadian Red Cross Memorial Hospital which has been unused since 1986.' (*Countryside Properties*: 24 October 2006.)

Exclusively for the over 55s, this fresh, 'new-age', emerging village is apparently sitting on a unique plot of Buckinghamshire supernatural history. The ghostly stories that have pervaded this 15-acre site in the Taplow area of the famous Cliveden estate are legion.

'Ghoulies and ghosties and long-leggedy beasties' have been claimed by many to have been former residents of the derelict and atmospheric abandoned Canadian Red Cross Memorial Hospital which was finally razed to the ground in 2006.

There is even a website 'shrine' dedicated to the history, haunting and death of what is affectionately known as the CRCMH or CRX for short. There are documented accounts by both ghost hunters and adventurous visitors to the abandoned hospital buildings, many of which describe the message that was scrawled at the southern end of the main corridor, '*WELCOME TO HELL*'.

This friendly greeting was backed up by other equally useful information such as '*The Green Lady comes if you knock 3 times.*' and '*Beware of the Bangee*'. The misspelling of Banshee, does little to lighten the tone. Perhaps they, whoever they are, really do mean '*Bangee*', given that the most notorious ghostly presence associated with this old hospital site was known as *the Flincher* whose arrival was heralded by an enormous bang, followed by a tremendous and powerful gust of reverberating air. Visitors to the derelict hospital preferred to whisper the name of this infamous and terrible ghost.

So let's go exploring this site – left derelict for 20 years prior to its 2006 re-incarnation as a new-age village – and learn what has really been experienced there, and who or what is – *sssshh* – the Flincher.

To set the scene – the origins of the hospital on the 376-acre Cliveden estate date back to 1914. The Astor family encouraged the Canadian Red Cross to set up a military hospital in the grounds at Taplow. This they did and called it the Duchess of Connaught Red Cross Hospital, and it was used by the Canadian Army Medical Corps. However, it was the development of this rather small facility in 1940 that led to a 'state of the art' hospital complex to serve the Canadian forces in the Second World War.

As the years passed the Canadian Red Cross Hospital went from strength to strength, turning into a specialist facility for research and the treatment of children with rheumatic conditions. It also became a famous maternity hospital and people all over the world can lay claim to having been born there. Many midwives and nurses also trained there after the war and into the 1980s. Like many such war-time constructions, the use of temporary Nissen-style huts became permanent.

It was a sprawling mix-and-match site, fronted by a grand sweeping entrance sporting colonial-style Doric columns, giving way to very basic brick buildings and rows of assorted outbuildings and huts.

Unfortunately, when the National Health Service took on the hospital after the war, the laboratory facilities were not expanded as progressively as they might have been and they remained fairly rudimentary. Budget cuts and a lack of political commitment to what was now an internationally recognised centre for immunology and rheumatology led to its decline and final closure in 1986. It then lay derelict until 2006 when it was demolished to make way for Cliveden village.

For the first few years of its closure, it was guarded and the curious were, on the whole, kept out. But from around 1988 onwards, it was an open house for any visitors who wanted to explore the wards, kitchens, the so-called Black Laboratories where animal experiments were conducted and the morgue. Indeed you could go wherever you liked, including the matron's office. It became a hospital version of the *Mary Celeste*.

It remained furnished with beds and the nurses' accommodation was still very habitable, as many travellers found. Also left behind were assorted spare parts and medical equipment, scattered X-rays and personal medical records left for all to see and vandalise. Riddled with aging roofing asbestos, it was a local safety hazard for any choosing fragile-roof-top play. Strangely, this was allowed to continue for a long time and local feeling ran high about the future of this 15-acre decaying complex containing danger and …'the Flincher'.

Reports were gathering apace about hauntings and a strange misty atmosphere that pervaded the extraordinarily long main hospital corridor. At an incredible 275 metres, it exceeded the length of an ocean liner such as the *Queen Mary*.

Eyewitness accounts of the first encounter with the Flincher came from musician Damon Torsten and artist Owen Pellow after they visited the derelict hospital in April 1994. Damon describes it well.

'There's this haze – a kind of aura around the place – and it can send a shiver down your spine. It's like someone or something telling you that you shouldn't be there. And the size of the group you're with doesn't change things, that feeling you're being watched, the eeriness of the lamp-post creaking and swaying on its fittings even though there is no breeze, the strange dripping noises and echoes around the buildings. There is no life within the hospital surrounds. You don't hear birds – anything you *can* hear is unfamiliar, like being in a different world. And it's a funny feeling. Like I said – almost comforting once you're in (especially if you're a regular visitor) – but for those first few minutes, you're truly on-edge. The hospital offers these warning signs during the daytime perhaps as a way of telling us all to get out of there by twilight. For at night, it becomes nobody's friend.'

17

There is such a consistent feeling by all who claim to have experienced something supernatural on the site – the contradictory mix of comfort with uneasiness and a feeling of being watched.

In April 1994 Owen Pellow and Damon Torsten were hoping to collect some more 'souvenirs' from the site. They had been quite taken aback by all the details they had previously discovered in a separate room – 'death files' – the precise and personal details of patients who had died at the hospital. They were intrigued to discover the details of Captain Turk, Royal Swanmaster to the Queen, who had died with a leg infection.

On this night-time visit they found it difficult to keep their torches alive despite having new batteries. They found themselves in what they described as a 'strangely angled passage', which they worked out would connect with the main corridor. It was littered with debris and was getting progressively darker as the torches faded to a flicker.

Then, as Damon says, it happened. 'Something broke the silence … and to this day I do not know what it was. There was a noise and we froze. A very *loud* noise – like nothing I'd heard before. A bang followed by sublime groaning – an ethereal roar of both bass and treble – an insane screeching that destroyed the tranquillity of the night … It appeared to emanate from somewhere around the very southern tip of the great corridor – maybe 30 metres from where we stood … Something was rushing towards us with incredible force – almost cyclonic. The only way I could sum this up was that it was like a million bats, or more accurately, the draught that might be created by a *gigantic* set of pounding bat wings coming our way. It wasn't just the noise, it was this instinctive feeling that something nasty was on its way. No, scratch that – not nasty – absolutely evil and terrifying. What was calm one moment turned suddenly into the most intensely *bad* emotional feeling I've ever had … The breeze changed and whatever it was was closing in on us. I could *feel* it, sense it getting nearer, and the nearer it got, the worse it felt. I don't know how many seconds we stood there glued to the floor, but I wager it couldn't have been many. However, it was long enough to know that what was happening was not a joke – it was all too incredibly real. Not only that, but whatever it was appeared to mean serious business. Deadly serious business. As soon as this had dawned on us, following seconds that had seemed like an eternity, we *bolted* out of there. Not just ran, but *RAN.*' They never looked back – they sometimes regret that they didn't, but hindsight is not a good judge – they knew that they had to flee and not stop until they were outside the grounds.

Damon went on, 'To explain this unexplainable entity, Owen coined the name "the Flincher" – something I'm hardly about to disagree with. But, what really was the Flincher? Was it a figment of our imagination. Most definitely not. Neither of us had been drinking and I can happily swear blind to this day that on that dark night – other than whatever entity we may have encountered – Owen and I, were the only living people at the Canadian Red Cross Memorial Hospital site in Taplow.'

Since that story emerged, the fad of 'urban exploring' gathered pace, targeting such abandoned sites across the UK, but it was the CRCMH (www.crcmh.com) that easily topped the 'supernatural charts' of such exploration.

I wanted to learn more about this extraordinary place, its atmosphere and haunted reputation, from others who had experienced it first-hand. It was clear from those I met that they had all felt such a sense of being in a supernatural environment and I judged it was a genuine response not an imagined, invoked reaction from being in a rather spooky place. For example, I recently spoke with Sandra who lived close to the hospital site, and like many locals became interested in the tale of the Flincher and other reports of a one-legged soldier on crutches slowly clumping along the northern corridors. In her explorations of the derelict site, together with her mum, dad and friends, they, like Damon and Owen, all got much more than they bargained for. This is best told in Sandra's own words which I think really capture the sense of actually being there.

She told me, 'My mum, dad and a few friends decided to do a séance in the chapel, not thinking anything of it because it would be this least likely place for activity as it was a place for grieving. My God, what a night. It was probably one of the scariest nights of my life. There were five of us, all joined hands, eyes closed, everything. One of the guys with us didn't join in, he stood and took photos.

'Nothing happened so we broke off and made our way out. We got outside ward 11 and four of us went in but my mum stayed outside.

'As we came back out, my mum started shouting, "Quick, quick take a picture, take a picture." The camera with new batteries decided to die and the corridor went absolutely ice cold, and my mum found she could not move – something was pinning her to the spot.

'We tried to go and walk down the corridor but realised she couldn't move and had also gone into a trance and started choking. It took about five minutes to move her away.

'One of the guys with us had to push her and pull her about, and this guy wasn't exactly the smallest in the world, far from it and he couldn't move her for love nor money. Finally we managed to sort it out but she was constantly being sick after and couldn't breathe and said, "I feel like someone has tried strangling me!" Whilst this was happening, the guy with the camera managed to get a picture from the side of her, but there was nothing there holding or stopping her, yet she was trapped.

'When the picture was checked on the digital camera, all I heard was "b***** hell", from the guy who took it. All I could see on the screen was a big ball of light enclosing the bottom half of her leg. We couldn't wait to get out of there, but before we left we realised we hadn't closed down the séance we had opened, so we all stood on the front entrance with everyone who had been in it in the first place and with the same guy taking photos. As we closed it down, it went cold again – bitter, I literally doubled over in pain. To this day I still do not know what it was! It felt like an electrical surge had gone through my stomach, almost as if I had been punched, but with electricity.

'When we got back and looked at the photos of the closing, little specks of light came from the centre of the ring of us. I was told they were orbs! It's really hard to explain, it was (still is) an unexplainable experience, almost unbelievable. But it happened.'

Like so many others who have visited this derelict hospital in search of the supernatural, there is a remarkable consistency in how they feel once inside the corridors or wards. Sandra summed it up well when she described it to me.

'The feeling in that place was amazing, safe but with an "on edge" feeling. I can't explain it, you feel like you are being followed or watched.'

Simon Cornwell's visit in December 2002, in search of The Flincher, was fraught with strange mists and fog blocking the camera, yet no such mist was visible to the eye. Exploring the infamous Black Labs, 'the spectral fog of doom', as he nicknamed it, kept reappearing, yet when he developed his pictures, it revealed a large orb exactly in the centre of the picture. He told me, 'Looking back on those pictures, there was something eerie and unexplained in those buildings: the blackened bath tubs, the blood in the kitchens, the carefully smashed doors and the grafitti which seemed to linger too long on 'green ladies' and ghostly images.'

Well now, the CRCMH is dead – but certainly not forgotten.

Former patients, surgical staff, nurses, doctors and ghost hunters alike still share the tales of a remarkable hospital – every nook and cranny logged and photographed. Spectral mists, glowing orbs, and mysterious shades captured in digital and moving images for those seeking evidence of the supernatural.

But now a new age dawns; the hospital dies, but a sparkling new village for the over-55s is born. In 2007, the BBC reported the estate agent for the new village as saying that many buyers had connections with the site. 'Lots of people who are interested have been local at some point', it was said.

Now take Mr Flincher at number 666 … My apologies, there was no mention of a Mr or Mrs Flincher in the BBC report, but who knows who may be living there now!

3

The Green Man of Hughenden

IT was a clear, bright September evening in 1986 as Mark Nursey drove to the Full Moon pub in Little Kingshill to meet his girlfriend Allyson Bulpett who was working there part-time.

He arrived around 9 pm, and Allyson, busy behind the bar, was pleased he had come. Mark thought it would be good to see her after work, even though they would be travelling home separately as Allyson had her own car parked at the pub.

Last orders were called and Mark, who was not drinking that evening, lent a hand with the clearing up.

By the time they were ready to go it was around 10.45 pm, so they set off, Allyson following Mark along Hare Lane. Mark recalls that evening as if it were yesterday, 'It was one of those really clear evenings, a full moon and the reflected light was fantastic.'

Empty roads lay ahead as they drove along Kingshill Road, then Cryer's Hill and turned left into the twisty Four Ashes Road. The moon illuminated the way ahead as they passed half a dozen or so bungalows, rounding the hedgerow bend that suddenly opens out to a large grassy area marking the beginning of Hughenden's landscaped cemetery.

As Mark came around towards the open space by the garden of rest he saw something that remains with him as vividly today as it was on that September night,

'There appeared to be this figure, it was a very distinctive figure and it was green.'

But it was much more than that. It stood nearly seven feet tall, and although this solid figure clearly had arms and legs, its green hue did not reveal any distinct hands or feet. But it was its head that was so striking. There were no defined facial features. It was glowing and very round, giving the appearance of a smoky green, translucent goldfish bowl.

The whole scene was as if frozen in time, yet it lasted only seconds. Mark drove on, looking into his rear view mirror to see Allyson's car as she also rounded the bend. She followed steadily behind, so he continued, his mind racing, wondering what on earth he had just witnessed.

As they approached their destination, a few miles on, Mark was flagged down by a distressed woman. Allyson saw it was a woman who often wandered around their road in a confused state and, knowing Mark would check that she was okay, she overtook him and got back to the flat first.

Mark came in shortly afterwards, explaining that the confused lady had wanted him to get something down from her loft. Mark had gently persuaded her to go home and he'd see to it another time.

This intervention had briefly diverted his mind from what had really pre-occupied him on the drive home, but the thoughts of the strange green figure soon returned. What an earth had he seen, he wondered.

However, Allyson turned to him first and said, 'Did you see that thing in Four Ashes Road?'

So it wasn't his imagination; with relief they realised they were both in awe of this strange apparition. Allyson had been taken aback by the misty, globe-like head with no facial features, yet with a solid green body.

Neither could quite understand the clear green detail of the torso, yet with undefined extremities that just ended in fuzziness.

Mark and Allyson knew, without a doubt, that they had both seen something 'other-worldly'. Was it a ghost? What on earth was it?

They both mentioned it to parents, family and friends who all said it must have just been the light playing tricks with their perception but they were in two separate cars, seeing exactly same thing half a minute apart from each other. This was a 'collective apparition' and a very powerful one indeed.

Bill Tilley, the editor of the *Bucks Free Press*, heard about Mark and Allyson's experience and found it all very convincing. He knew that there was a long folklore tradition linking a host of related unexplained phenomena such as green men, ley lines and other spiritual energies. Many historic pubs in areas where sightings have been claimed are actually called the Green Man, and Buckinghamshire hosts several of these, including one in nearby Prestwood.

After some research the *South Bucks Star* published an account of Mark and Allyson's sighting under the headline 'The Green Man of Hughenden'. The paper described the whole incident and then went on to explore what might lie behind it.

'One theory', it claimed, 'is that the figure was a spirit of the forest, a green man, as depicted on a number of pub signs in the Chilterns.' The article went on to claim that 'a green man is also said to haunt the woods at Fingest. Another clue to his appearance may be a ley line passing near the haunted spot. Ley lines – alignments of ancient sites such as churches, stone circles and holy wells – are thought, by some, to possess mysterious powers.' (*South Bucks Star,* 26 September 1986.)

It was also of interest that an organisation at the time called the Strange Folklore Society from High Wycombe was researching a ley line that, it was claimed, actually started in the area of Four Ashes Road.

Reading about Mark and Allyson's experience in the *Star,* local warehouseman Phil Mullett was taken aback by the account. Eight years previously, he had seen exactly the same apparition at the same spot, but had said nothing about it.

He told the *Star,* 'It gave me quite a shock to read it. The account was so close to my own. It was about 9.30 pm when I drove into Four Ashes Road and on turning my car lights on full, I saw this green person appear from the right-hand side of the road. It drifted out to the centre of the road and turned towards me. It waved its arms, not to frighten, but as if to warn me to keep back. It drifted into the hedge on the other side of the road but as I got closer it came out again to the centre, turned and lifted its arms. I knew I was going to hit it. I think I cried out or shouted something.' (*South Bucks Star,* 17 October 1986.)

Slamming on his brakes he could not stop before hitting the seven-foot tall green figure. Shaking, he got out the car but there was nothing there. No figure, no sign at all of anything on the road. He carried this frightening incident with him for eight years before realising that others had seen exactly the same apparition.

What really puzzled Phil was the fact that although it had a solid-looking body, the hands and legs were not clearly defined. However, it was the face – or, rather, lack of a face – that really stuck with him. He said that where the face should be was just a misty, round, grey shape. Phil had seen exactly the same figure as Mark and Allyson, but eight years earlier.

When I spoke with Mark Nursey – a down-to-earth, straight-talking fireman – he was in no doubt about what he saw and no amount of leg-pulling from his colleagues would dissuade him from describing that September night's experience.

What was interesting, also, was the fact that this had occurred 22 years previously, the newspaper article of the time long ago lost and forgotten by Mark. When I contacted him 'out of the blue' researching for this book, his account was identical to earlier stories.

'I can remember it as if it were yesterday – I really can,' he told me. It was clear that Mark really meant it and he felt quite spooked talking about it again after all this time.

Allyson Bulpett also spoke with me, and equally startling was her recollection of that same experience – again it was both their vivid memories of the misty, rounded, goldfish-bowl-like head where a face should be that was so striking. Also interesting was that they were both unaware of the article in the *Star* in October of that same year about Phil Mullett's experience eight years before. So, just as

Phil was relieved to not be alone in having seen the green apparition, both Mark and Allyson were fascinated to learn that they were not the first ones to have witnessed the same supernatural experience all those years ago.

But was it a supernatural experience? What other evidence do we have that can explain it? Daphne Phillips' research into the Green Man of Fingest reveals a 14th-century legend revolving around a certain bishop, Henry Burghersh, and his falling out with the villagers of the Manor of Fingest over the sequestration of over 300 acres of their common land for his own park and woodland hunting pleasures, leaving them little over 100 acres for their livelihood. To say he was disliked by the locals was an understatement and no tears were shed when he died around 1343.

However, his ghost was said to return as a forest 'keeper' dressed in green to put right his misdeeds. He is claimed to have said to a certain squire of the village that he had offended God and injured the poor by his actions and was doomed to be the keeper of the park until it was put back in the hands of the villagers (Daphne Phillips, 'The Green Man of Fingest', in *Strange Wycombe* by Alan Cleaver).

Arguments continue today about this historical incident, and so do claimed sightings. Whether in a green cloak or strange hat or green tunic, the witnesses claim that he appears in the churchyard of St Bartholomew's begging passers-by to restore the commoners' lands so he can rest in peace. Others say that he roams the woodlands around the village.

The legend does not offer very much insight into the Hughenden incidents but does confirm a long tradition across the centuries and across the world of the depiction of 'green knights, green huntsmen' and green 'wild' men of the woods that have some kind of moral or protective role. (The original Green Man is said to be the Celtic god Cernunnos, as depicted by the Gundestrup Cup in Copenhagen's National Museum.) Others see them as connected to ancient fertility rites and integral to the true spirit of nature – nature's supernatural presence perhaps?

Most researchers into Green Men – and there are many – attribute academic and folklore researcher Lady Raglan as being responsible for giving life to the whole concept by coining the very name 'Green Man' in a 1939 article for *Folklore* magazine entitled 'The Green Man in Church Architecture' (Lady Raglan, *Folklore*, Vol. 50, March 1939). She was intrigued by carvings commonly found in churches, of what are termed 'foliate heads' – heads with intertwined leaves for hair and beards. Some are so complex that only close inspection of what appears to be an intricate foliage design reveals a man's head. Very occasionally a 'green woman' is depicted. Why are they so popular? Do (or did) such entities exist?

They are seen by some researchers as our most primitive supernatural selves, perhaps ghosts of our pagan past. Alongside the Green Man label Lady Raglan also referred to them as 'wild men'.

In his book *The Green Man: A Field Guide* (Compass Books 2000) Clive Hicks believes such wild men '… are not necessarily malevolent and are depicted as helping humanity in some cases. The wild man represents an asset in each of us, the whole reservoir of qualities with which each of us is endowed.'

Researcher Gary Varner asks, 'Do these mythical wild men exist? I believe so. They are part of the myths of nature and appear at times of stress in the world. It may not be an everyday event, but they exist in two worlds at separate times. They are part of the Green Man spirit and act and react to protect the small wilderness that is left in this teeming world.' (Varner, GR, *The Mythology of the Green Man*, 2007.)

Ask Mark, Allyson and Phil if they exist – they will certainly confirm that at least a Green Man of Hughenden most certainly does.

4

Supernatural Apparitions and the Haddenham Warning

IF we regard ghosts as a form of residual 'memory', perhaps a supernatural essence that has somehow become part of the fabric of a certain location, hauntings can be seen to take on a purposeful role, providing a warning of danger, death or impending disaster – or maybe they are merely manifestations of spirits unable to let go of their earthly origins.

Our contemporary world engages in the storage of data which would have been beyond the imagination of our recent ancestors. We clutch images, words and music in small electronic cards or memory sticks ready to be revived at any time. The speed of technological advance is such that we know that what we are purchasing is becoming old technology as we buy it. Eventually we are to become the ancestors of those who will claim that what they are capable of hearing, seeing, doing was beyond *our* wildest imagination.

But I wager there will still be hauntings and ghosts, visions and apparitions – a sort of supernatural 'wire-less technology' that remains beyond the realm of natural explanation and provides spiritual versions of stored memories much like those we currently capture electronically and scientifically. Possibly someone reading this right now will be that haunting, or ghost, or apparition. Will it be you?

One of the most frequently experienced apparitions is that of someone known to the observer, or that of a pet, such as a dog or cat. Known as 'crisis apparitions', they are, unfortunately, associated with the immediate danger or imminent death of the subject of the vision. Time and time again, across the world, reports are collated describing how close friends or relatives have been seen, but in the wrong place at the wrong time. Perhaps standing at the foot of the bed when they are living hundreds of miles away, or watching from across a busy street, when they are in fact ill in hospital or living in another country.

The person who experiences the apparition then later discovers that the person they saw had died very close to, or even at the same time as, their supernatural appearance.

It seems to be encapsulated in a time-frame of approximately twelve hours before death occurs, right through to twelve hours after death. So at any time during that crucial 24-hour period, often at the very time of death, the crisis apparition is seen. Sometimes called 'ghosts of the living', they generally appear only once and rarely become a haunting or residual memory in that location. This form of short-term apparition is very personal and, in the main, very loving – as a last farewell to those they are leaving behind. Occasionally, however, the danger passes, the troubled person survives and the story is told and re-told.

The case of James, a 21-year-old sales executive in Cryers Hill, is typical of what can occur and is a very clear example of how a crisis apparition works. In March 2005 James was asleep in bed until he was startled by a bright light shining through the doorway at around 11.30 pm. He recalls sitting up and being frozen to the spot as the light took on the shape of a person. Although it lasted a mere fifteen seconds, the figure seemed to be looking towards him. He found the courage to get up and turn on his bedroom light but nothing was to be seen and there were no other lights on the landing or in the rest of the house. He could not explain where this light had appeared from at all.

The next morning the news reached him.

James's grandmother had been killed in a car accident in Ireland at around 11 pm that same night. She was very fond of her grandson and James is convinced that she was paying a last visit. This does fit all the evidence we have of such occurrences. It has been explained by some as a form of telepathy, whereby the brain pattern signals from the distressed and injured person are so powerful they can reach across vast distances to trigger a response in a loved one. What is more natural than a grandmother's energy in this last terrible moment focusing on thoughts of her grandson and wanting to see him perhaps for the last time. He in turn tunes into this powerful telepathic signal without even realising it.

The brain then attempts to convert this signal into a recognisable image. In some cases the image is crystal clear – the person is there before you; in other situations, such as that confronting James, it is indicative rather than absolute, but the receiver knows who it is. It is personal, special and identifiable. James knows his gran said goodbye.

Animals can also be seen in a similar manner via a crisis apparition and this can signal that the friend or relative who owns the pet is in trouble, or indeed, the animal itself has died. My only personal experience of this was a night-time telephone call from my mother to say she was very puzzled, having been woken up by Gina, the family Airedale, sitting bolt upright on her bed. When she reached forward to touch her, the dog vanished.

At that time, Gina, who had spent many happy times with my mum and dad although she belonged to my wife's family, had moved out to Malta with my in-laws some years previously. My mother was concerned that somehow Gina had found her way back to Stoke Poges. Logic said it was impossible, but she was there as clear as day and we knew she always got excited in the car heading out to my parents' house. In fact my wife and I would try to trick her by finding different routes but she would stand up within a mile of arrival, bark and wag her tail furiously. So was it possible she had made such an amazing journey?

I telephoned Malta immediately only to discover that Gina had died at the same time that my mother had seen her appear in the bedroom. In fact, my call had interrupted my in-laws who were trying to decide on the best way to break the news to their daughter and to me.

The most famous Buckinghamshire case of a 'crisis apparition' is that of William Edden. The tale dates from 1828 but remains relevant today because the apparition concerned was far from transitory and can occasionally be seen in the Haddenham area where Edden met a violent, murderous death by pole-axe. It is claimed that this residual memory aimed to warn other travellers but now has become caught in a form of supernatural time warp that triggers the distraught image to re-appear sporadically to those passing the scene of his death.

The market gardener, known locally as Noble Edden rather than William Edden, actually lived in Thame just over the border in Oxfordshire. He was found brutally clubbed to death on the Aylesbury road, not too far from what was then the Cider House pub at Haddenham where his body was taken for the inquest, which ruled he had been murdered 'by some person or persons unknown'. Mrs Edden, however, knew something terrible had happened to her husband, and she is recorded as saying, 'When I was ironing a shirt on the Saturday night my husband was murdered – something came over me – and I thought my husband came by me. I looked up and thought I heard the voice of my husband come from near my mahogany table as I turned from my ironing. I ran out and said, "Oh Dear God! My husband is murdered, and his ribs are broken!" I told this to several of my neighbours. Mrs Chester was the first to whom I told it. I mentioned it also at the Saracen's Head.' (*The Times*, 31 August 1829.)

Indeed, the investigating surgeons, Mr Reynolds from Thame and Mr Lee from Haddenham, did discover 'five ribs beaten in'. The broken ribs had penetrated and ruptured Edden's liver. The police discovered the murder weapon to be a monstrous two-foot-long pole-axe with a hammer head on one side and sharp axe on the other.

At the trial of Benjamin Tyler, one of the murder suspects, Mrs

Edden was asked, 'Have you any objection to say why you thought your husband was murdered?'

'No,' replied Mrs Edden, 'I thought I saw my husband's apparition and the man that done it; and that man was Tyler.'

She was also asked, 'What made you think that your husband's ribs were broken?' To which she replied, 'I saw a hammer, or something like a hammer and it came into my mind that his ribs are broken.'

This was a remarkable case given that all the details of Mrs Edden's crisis apparition turned out to be true and are documented as such in court records of the murder trial. Yet there was no way she could have known these details or events from any third party prior to her making them public. Indeed, she had organised ten local men led by James Mears to set off to search for her husband around 10 pm that same night, such was her strong vision of his murder. They came across his cart on the roadside, shafts in the air, the harness still there but no horse and more importantly, no Noble Edden. He had already been discovered by other travellers who had taken him to the Cider House in a wheelbarrow for the post-mortem.

This murder took place on Saturday, 25 October 1828 sometime between 5 pm and 6.30 pm and leads us into another realm of contemporary hauntings known as anniversary ghosts.

If you can pinpoint the exact murder location for that October date (approximately one mile from the Bottle and Glass pub in Gibraltar going towards Haddenham just before the right turn towards Cuddington) and you are attuned to the story of that terrible evening, it is said you will feel the presence of this dark deed through a massive temperature drop, pressure on your rib-cage and possibly a crisis apparition of Noble Edden himself – a supernatural sign of impending doom.

If this should happen to you, just remember that the Bottle and Glass pub is only a mile away and four minutes is still the accepted measure for amateur milers!

5

A Buckinghamshire Supernatural Pub Crawl

Pubs and taverns always seem to predominate when it comes to supernatural stories and Buckinghamshire is no exception. In fact so many public houses across the county claim to be haunted, it would be unusual to find a pub without a ghost or two.

It is not surprising that they should feature so often given their important role in bringing people together for pleasurable social interaction and playing host to a whole variety of travellers passing through their doors. Fables, tales and folklore are swapped and embroidered there, becoming close literary companions to that of alcohol consumption and friends well met. 'Tis true, as I am standing here. Over in that corner, he stood, all dressed in black and just starin' at me.'

Snatched conversations can often deliver up such titbits to 'prove' the raconteur's veracity. What started as a ghost story for a stormy winter's night in front of a blazing log fire can, over the years, turn into a true story that happened to 'old Bill' who unfortunately has now passed away, unable to verify his terrifying experience with a whirling dervish in the snug, whilst a full moon shone outside.

I did, however, discover a clutch of tales that do seem to be based on real, first-hand experiences rather than distant stories retold. So settle down by the bar for some supernatural stories of Buckinghamshire public houses.

Oh, thanks – very kind – mine's a pint of best.

Ghostly Aperitifs

Well-known local writer and broadcaster John Pilgrim – experienced and very adept at story-telling himself – kicks off our supernatural pub crawl in Edlesborough with a gentle, thought-provoking, true tale.

The village itself is a wonderfully atmospheric place dominated by the 13th-century St Mary's church. It is said to lie directly on 'the Dragon Line', a famous ley line connecting significant monuments, villages and churches right across the country, and to be associated with supernatural events such as ghost sightings.

With the legend of the highwayman Dick Turpin, who supposedly is still to be seen galloping furiously to his hideout in nearby Butler's Manor, the area holds an supernatural feel that John soon found to be real.

During the 1980s John and his wife Margaret ran the Bell pub just opposite the church. (The combination of church and pub is a wonderful feature of English villages, the latter able to supply the former with regular sinners.) There was alleged to be a secret tunnel from the pub to the church although John never found it.

There proved to be a slightly scary start to their new life as publicans, not through supernatural causes, but because of the terror caused across the region by the notorious violent rapist and burglar nicknamed the Fox who had, by August 1984, repeated his terrible crimes in Edlesborough.

John told me, 'I decided that I would move into the pub on my own because the infamous 'Fox' was committing offences in the area. Thankfully he was arrested just before we were due to move in.'

With verve and enthusiasm, John and Margaret worked hard to settle in and they created a popular pub for both locals and visitors to this historic village. Shortly after moving in, John invited his sister Linda to come and view her brother's latest venture. She had not been party to John and Margaret's plan to run a pub but knowing John like she did, she wasn't too surprised he'd decided to do such a thing. He's a character who has a long list of ambitions to achieve and was determined to tick them off rather than just talk about them, and here was John 'Landlord' Pilgrim embarking on his latest adventure with his beloved.

Whilst Linda was not taken aback by her brother's new persona, John certainly was by Linda's first question to him on the day she arrived. Linda told me, 'I said to John, "Where's the broom John?" and he said, "What broom?" I said, "There's a girl in there looking for a broom." John said, "There is no girl, what on earth are you talking about?" '

Linda explained that when she came in there was a young girl by the fireplace; she was sweeping up leaves with an old-fashioned besom broom, leaves that had blown in the pub with the autumn winds, and she was saying, 'Where's the broom? Where's the broom?' Linda also knew, although unsure how, that the missing broom was supposed to be by the fireplace.

John knew his sister was not prone to such imaginings and asked the regulars, who confirmed that such a spirit had been seen by others in the pub, including the previous owners who were responsible for uncovering the original inglenook fireplace. His sister had no prior knowledge of this and her sighting matched those of the earlier ones of a young servant girl. From this time onwards, John always acknowledged her by nodding 'hallo' towards the fireplace even though he couldn't see her.

'Who is she and will I ever see her myself?' he wondered. It seems, however, that the sensitive canine ability of one of their dogs had already had that privilege.

'We owned two dogs when we were in the Bell, a Dalmatian called Luke and a mongrel called Pippa. Luke often went potty when he entered the saloon bar where the ghost was supposed to be,' recalls John.

John then recounts that one morning around 7.30 am he was bringing logs into the bar for the fire and he was kneeling down, stacking them to the side ready for use later in the day.

'Morning guvnor, it's pretty chilly aint it?'

Startled, John turned around to see, not a young girl, in fact just the opposite. Sitting at the bar gazing directly at him was an elderly lady.

He was puzzled as to how on earth she had entered the bar without him seeing her, especially as she did not look too fast on her feet. She had just appeared as if out of the blue.

Over a cup of tea, John managed to find out she was living in a nearby residential home and had wandered off, so he arranged for her to be collected and taken back. So not the ghost after all, but there was one curious piece of information that John discovered. As a young girl, she had been a cleaner at that very pub and one of her jobs was to sweep that very fireplace.

Wishful thinking can be a powerful mental force when you are elderly, and thinking back about the old times. How often she must have conjured up such memories in her mind's-eye. Perhaps these images were more powerful than even she could have realised and the eyes of others, such as Linda, might occasionally have glimpsed her young-self, transported back to her earlier life.

Astral projection can create 'living ghosts' and the astral plane is not bound by the passing of the years. Even more intriguing is the possibility of a 'time-slip'. Instead of the ghost being out of its time, it is the witness who is. In this case it was Linda who, momentarily, was in the wrong dimension when some kind of portal opened up. Linda had not only seen her sweeping leaves with that besom broom, but she told me there was an old flagstone floor rather than the actual carpeted one. This would suggest that Linda was the 'ghost' in the girl's time rather than vice-versa.

Far-fetched perhaps, but either way – real ghost or 'living ghost' – it is an intriguing supernatural conundrum from John Pilgrim.

*****

The Lovesick Ghost

We leave the Bell in Edlesborough to visit the Duck in Bedgrove near Aylesbury where, according to a medium called Dee, there is a love-stricken ghost. The only problem is that he's fallen in love with the very human barmaid.

It was in 2004 that the manager of that time, Graham Gray, and his partner Jo Ward were startled to see a collective apparition. In supernatural terms, if two people manage to see the same spiritual presence it is called a 'collective apparition' and carries much more weight in terms of convincing the sceptics.

Jo described to *The Bucks Herald* how she had seen a ghostly figure of a man, all in black, standing at the bar. Graham had also seen the figure that just vanishes if approached or spoken to. Customers have also reported a cold presence close to them at the bar.

When they took over the pub in December 2003, Jo and Graham reported a feeling of being watched and hearing crates being dragged across the cellar floor. Indeed, in the morning, a visit to the cellar would reveal just that – full crates that had been dragged to another position and on one occasion a crate had been lifted to the top of the cellar stairs and could have caused a serious accident. Jo and the bar staff have also heard a high pitched scream.

Jo told the press, 'It really freaked us out and just minutes later, the fire alarm went off for the third time that week without explanation ….' (*The Bucks Herald,* 18 February 2004.)

A month later, after more noises and appearances by the man in black, Graham and Jo invited local medium Dee to try and discover who their ghostly visitor might be and what he wanted. He had now taken to moving the football trophies on the shelf behind the bar and still dragged crates across the cellar floor.

Dee confirmed that there was something spiritual residing in their pub. She then said that the man, whose name was Chris, had been executed by hanging on that very site in the 19th century, that he was 22 and had worked as a farm labourer. According to Dee, he is stuck on this side of life looking for his companion called James who was also executed (*The Bucks Herald,* 23 March 2004).

There was no indication of what they had done to be executed, but at that time minor acts of theft, forgery and related crimes carried the death penalty. Nearby Aylesbury was a major assize town and, although the site of the Duck pub would have been farmland belonging to Bedgrove Farm in the 19th century, my research shows that the visiting judge was in the habit of stopping in his carriage under an enormous elm tree near this place, around the Westmorland Avenue area, then known as Great Tree Road. Here his carriage would be met by the High Sheriff's carriage from Aylesbury, and a local farm lad would place a bale of straw on the track between the two carriages as they drew up side by side. The judge would then transfer from his carriage into the High Sheriff's without setting foot directly upon the road (*South Bucks Free Press,* 18 May 1883).

Hardly supernatural, of course, but it is interesting that this same area was one of local importance and judicial ceremony and, no doubt, other more dubious acts given the symbolic nature of the great elm for a variety of nefarious meetings. It is not clear if hangings took place here, but certainly there was a ready-made gibbet should it be needed. It is possible that it also doubled as a crossroads where executed felons were buried. Also people who committed suicide were routinely buried at crossroads; some county customs demanded a stake be hammered into the heart to prevent them from haunting the locality.

The shock revelation for everybody, however, was when Chris told Dee he had fallen in love with Jo and liked being at the bar where he could gaze at her. She has since left, but Chris still makes his presence known.

Graham said, 'I never believed in ghosts before and would laugh about them – but I definitely believe in the supernatural now.' (*The Bucks Herald,* 18 February 2004.)

*****

Scents and Sounds
Also believing in the supernatural is Simon Kemp, a bar assistant at the Boot and Slipper pub in Amersham on the Hill. Although no one has seen a ghost, to some extent it would be preferable if they

had because instead of an apparition, you are likely to feel a cold hand grasp your shoulder. The problem is that no one is there when it happens to you. Also something has a habit of 'brushing past' with impatient muttering noises when you are entering the cellar. Going down to the cellar is not part of the job that any of the bar staff look forward to (*Bucks Free Press* 25 January 2001).

This aspect of the supernatural is very common – no actual ghost appears but there is a distinct feeling of a presence with a definite, measurable, cold atmosphere, a feeling of being watched and then perhaps a slight touch or breeze as it passes you by and possibly you might hear a slight murmur or mutter. All senses are capable of picking up a supernatural presence. Often there is a smell known as the olfactic factor – a sudden smell of violets or lavender, a sweet perfume or perhaps a cigarette, cigar or pipe smell where there shouldn't be one. My wife and daughter both experienced this after my father died – as they came in the front door together, they both turned to each other, startled, and in unison, said 'Grandpa'. The smell of Manikin cigars in the hallway was overwhelming – his favourite tobacco – yet he had never smoked them in this house.

Pubs contain so many conflicting smells that it is difficult to isolate the olfactic factors, although they could well be present. The recent ban on smoking in pubs could well lead to more people noticing such things but, on the whole, it is the sense of touch and temperature that predominates, together with audible features such as footsteps or items being dragged along.

For example, the Greyhound Inn at Akeley, near Buckingham regularly echoed to the sound of footsteps upstairs. The problem was that not only was there no one upstairs, at least no human, but the footsteps managed to move into different bedrooms despite closed doors and partition walls. For the landlady who first reported this throughout the 1950s, Mrs Violet Cowley, it would only happen during the afternoon when the pub was closed. It was a regular afternoon occurrence but when she or her daughter went upstairs to look, no one was to be seen. Violet could also hear murmured conversations but again no one was there.

Architecturally, this Elizabethan coaching inn contains a priest's hole and there used to be a different configuration of upstairs bedrooms with their own independent staircase, loft area and bakehouse. The ghostly footsteps were following the old layout which took them through what were now walled areas.

I spoke with Mrs Cowley, now in her late 80s, and as bright as a button. She recalled all of the above experiences as something never to be forgotten. I also met her son John whose bedroom contained the priest's hole.

'Whether it was ghosts or not I don't know but you could wake up in the night and look towards the door in the wall and you'd see like a pair of mice eyes going down the wall, and I often thought well, there's a lot of mice in here, and I used to get out of bed and turn the light on but there was nothing there. It was like a pair of bright eyes starting near the ceiling and moving down the wall – it used to scare me something chronic but I never did tell mum.'

*****

Supernatural Spirits in Amersham

If you see something supernatural other than an apparition, then it is often that items have been moved around in a room, or perhaps objects disappear and re-appear somewhere else. Pets are great indicators of supernatural atmospheres, often refusing to enter certain rooms, corners or hallways, exhibiting both fear and curiosity – staring intently at the area of concern to them.

Buttock pinching, however, is a pretty direct way to get attention. Michelle Roberts is one of the bar staff at the Elephant and Castle pub in old Amersham, who has experienced an unseen hand pinching her bottom.

She told local reporters, 'I went down into the cellar to get some drinks and then I felt my bottom being pinched – I had heard stories about it before I came to work here – and I just dropped the bottles and ran out. I was a bit shocked.' (*Bucks Free Press*, 25 January 2001.)

Sylvia Shippey, landlady at the time, has said that her son and her neighbour have both seen a woman dressed totally in black appear in the kitchen of the flat above the pub and just melt through the walls. Is it she who is pinching bar-staff's bottoms? Or is there another entity down in the cellar?

Old Amersham is replete with tales of pub ghosts – it seems to be the epicentre for such apparitions and supernatural events. The Crown, originally a 16th-century coaching inn, found fame in 1994 by featuring its historic four-poster bedroom where Charles (Hugh Grant) and Carrie (Andie MacDowell) spent a passionate night in Mike Newell's film, *Four Weddings and a Funeral*. Had they really spent the night there they may have stumbled across one of the alleged five resident ghosts.

Margaret Wingrove who worked there found it very amusing to meet guests, particularly young men, as they fled from their room after a Victorian housekeeper insisted on tucking them in, in the early hours of the morning – a warm gesture from a very cold apparition that wouldn't take no for an answer.

She reported other guests waking suddenly, feeling that an electric shock had passed through their body. One particular ghostly resident seems to have taken exception to a recent extension, and according to Margaret, shouts 'Get out now!' Needless to say, it tends to get its own way (*Bucks Free Press*, 25 January 2001)

Before leaving old Amersham, it is the Chequers pub that holds the record as the most haunted public house in the village. This is one of the most investigated pubs because of the occasion in 1521 when it was used to imprison six religious martyrs on the night before they were burnt at the stake in nearby Rectory Woods.

The Lollard Dissenters were both a political and a religious movement that first emerged in the mid 14th century based on the powerful teachings of a leading Oxford University theologian, John Wyclif (c1330–1384), who challenged the authority of the priests. He claimed that the poorest, most humble villager had as much authority as a priest when it came to religious rites, as they were

41

truly pious, but priests were often far from being so. Seen by the Church as anticlerical and heretical, the Lollards faced prosecution and risked being burnt at the stake like witches. In Buckinghamshire it was Robert Cheyne, famously associated with the building of Chesham Bois House, who was under suspicion in the 16th century. However, whilst he survived investigation, six local Lollard men and one woman did not. The dreadful fate that was to befall all of them was first carried out on one Amersham Dissenter, William Tylsworth, who was burnt at the stake in 1511. (The Martyrs' Memorial says 1506; however, later research by the Amersham Museum has discovered that this terrible event was carried out in 1511.) But if this was not cruel enough, Tylsworth's married daughter, Joan Clark, was forced to begin his terrible, torturous death by lighting the faggots stacked around his legs.

It was thought that this horrific spectacle would compel others to repent their support for Lollardy but it did not. Others across the county were burnt and even strangled, but in Amersham itself it is the imprisoning and execution by burning in 1521 of five men and one woman that is still said to reverberate in supernatural anguish today. Again in the case of one man, John Scrivener, his young children were ordered to light the faggots with the fire that would consume their father.

A monument now stands to one side of a shallow depression on the soil where now a total of seven men and one woman died for their beliefs. Some people claim to have witnessed figures dressed in 16th-century clothing in that vicinity. However, it is at the site of the Chequers pub in the old village where their cries of anguish are still allegedly heard.

Over the years reports include not only moaning and screaming noises, but also the appearance of a white hooded figure. For no apparent reason, dogs can become 'spooked' by the atmosphere in certain unexplained cold spots. Mediums called to the pub have indicated the presence of a warder or custodian called Auden, claimed to be the gaoler of the Amersham Martyrs, who is now trapped this side of life in anguish at what he has done.

So seriously have various occupants of the Chequers been troubled by the hauntings over the years, that it has been exorcised at least three times. In her book *Ghosts of Buckinghamshire* (Countryside Books, 1995) Betty Puttick relates that although the pub was exorcised in 1953, the trouble soon started up again when a new landlord took over 10 years later. His daughters, aged 8 and 11, screamed in terror, sobbing as they blurted out to their concerned father who had rushed to their bedroom that a white hooded figure had drifted around their room and out through the door.

Thus began a period of closed doors opening and the return of moaning and screaming. By 1964, after a medium had identified at least one ghost – Auden – a clergyman was called in to exorcise the pub once more.

It seems around a decade or so passes, then, perhaps coinciding with new owners, the disturbance starts again as indeed it did in the 1980s when once more an exorcism took place.

I visited the pub in February 2008, and the regulars seemed quite used to experiencing unexplained events in the public bar area. Landlord Bob Pugsley even caught the last one on a CCTV security camera. A pint glass standing on the bar spontaneously shattered leaving just a perfect top rim. A real puzzle as nowadays the glasses are made of safety glass that is difficult to break even when thrown. A salad bowl did exactly the same, as if it had been subjected to some extraordinary invisible pressure. This is typical of spirit energy making itself known to the living. Something is still causing supernatural waves in the Chequers – but who or what?

Local chiropodist and podiatrist Diana Canning may hold the answer. Also qualified as a legal expert witness, she is someone used to finding medical, scientific or logical explanations rather than fanciful speculative ones, let alone supernatural causes. Some years ago, Diana was asked by the landlady of the time if she would kindly call in to treat her elderly mother who was not mobile enough to visit the clinic. Diana agreed and a few days later called at the busy pub. She was shown up the narrow staircase to the elderly lady's bedroom.

Diana was introduced to the landlady's mother and they both assisted her into her favourite chair ready for her chiropody session. Making sure Diana was all set, the landlady went back downstairs to the pub. Meanwhile, Diana had laid out all her equipment in her own special order of use on a chest of drawers just beside her. Being very methodical she placed them precisely so that she could reach out without looking to grasp the correct instrument for each part of her delicate work on the patient's feet.

Diana told me, 'I was talking to the old lady and I thought this room is so cold, although it did not strike me as being cold when I went in. I thought this is so cold, unnaturally cold for an old person.'

Diana asked her if she wanted a blanket around her, but the elderly lady said she was fine, not cold at all. Diana was about to begin treating the lady's feet but sensed that someone was standing behind her. This is not unusual, a member of the family often comes in to ask if there is anything she needs like a flannel, towels or even a cup of tea perhaps. At the moment of sensing that someone was behind her, she was tapped on the shoulder so firmly that she could hear the noise – the fingers made a very distinct, audible tap.

She turned around immediately expecting to see the old lady's daughter but there was no one there at all. Then Diana felt someone or something invisible pass her – a very definite but light brushing sensation. Whoever had tapped her on the shoulder was now pushing past her. The elderly lady was quite undisturbed and Diana, feeling a little confused by these sensations, decided to say nothing but to just carry on and begin the treatment. When she reached out to get one of her instruments, instead of being where she had carefully and systematically laid them out, ready to hand, they had all been moved along so they no longer matched her regular working pattern.

She now knew something very strange was happening. Her instruments had without any doubt been moved. But how? Why? Rather than disturb her new patient with her thoughts, she finished the session and bade her goodbye. The landlady thanked her and said she would call by the clinic as usual next week.

The following week, the landlady called at Diana's clinic and said how good it had been of her to call and treat her mother, but she had noticed that Diana looked a little shaken when she had left the pub but she hadn't wanted to mention it in case it was her imagination. Diana told the landlady what had happened. The landlady then confessed that the pub was haunted and that the apparition of a woman in white occasionally appeared in her mother's bedroom and had just returned the day before Diana's visit. She said that everything went very cold, and that is when they knew she was back. The events Diana described were typical.

Diana of course hadn't actually seen her but the elderly lady and her daughter had. She associated the apparition with the Amersham Martyrs, one of whom was a woman. There is no evidence, however, that the ghost was Joan Norman, held at the pub prior to her execution with her companion Lollards. Whatever her identity, she is still seeking attention perhaps to tell her story somehow, some day.

The landlady apologised to Diana and said, 'I was going to tell you, then I thought better of it, then I totally forgot.'

One thing was very certain, Diana never forgot and never went back.

*****

Lingering Legendary Spiritual Liqueurs in the Chalfonts
There is an important connection between these events reported at the Chequers and two other historic inns just outside the town of Amersham. One is the Ivy House – a tavern en route to Aylesbury and Oxford from London which became famous for its stabling and excellent facilities for travellers. The other is the Greyhound Inn in Chalfont St Peter. A formidable judicial history reverberates here since its close association with the infamous hanging judge, Judge Jeffreys (c1648–1689).

When I met Audrey Barrett, manager at the Ivy House, she explained, 'They used to drop the prisoners at the Chequers and come and stable the horses and carriages here, and then they used to take them on to the Greyhound the next day to the hanging judge.'

The Ivy House does retain a strong supernatural connection with stabling and resting the horses. Apparently a young stable lad died when he tripped and was trampled by horses. To this day he is still to be seen upstairs at the Ivy House where some servants' attic rooms used to be.

I wanted to check this story out to see if anyone has experienced this supernatural association. I spoke some more with Audrey to discover what she felt about this claim of a ghost at the Ivy House.

'What can I say?' she mused. 'When I first came here eight years ago I didn't believe in ghosts but I do now. The toilets used to be upstairs and my office used to be next door. Whenever I was in my office I used to get a feeling that somebody was watching me or I'd hear footsteps along the corridor, you'd turn around and there was nobody there and the toilet doors had not been opened or closed. Also you'd walk up the stairs – and the first set of stairs that you went up you went through an absolutely icy patch and then it would be hot again and you'd think why is that? We all used to say he'd be sitting there to watch us.'

Who is he? I needed to know. It appears that Jane, Audrey's colleague, now knows. The toilet and office area that Audrey referred to has now been totally refurbished as guest rooms, yet within that same area something supernatural is definitely happening.

Jane told me, 'I always catch him out of the corner of my eye. He just stands there.'

'Where are you when this happens?' I asked.

'Mostly on the stairs or I've just come out of a bedroom. I have actually looked straight at him and he's just been stood there, this dark haired young man, bless him.'

'How old?' I inquired.

'I'd say about 15 or 16. He's not very old – he might be older but I don't think he is. He has short dark hair, very dirty looking, very scruffy and really tatty clothes with a waistcoat type thing on with a shirt. I was just stunned by the fact that he was there. His face is very, very pale, he just looked at me then "poof" gone. It's only happened the once but I always know when he's around because I get cold air swirl round me.'

Audrey and Jane explained that his name is Sam, not because they know that's his name, but because the previous owners were well aware of the same haunting presence and one day they discovered a picture had fallen over and on the back in the dust was etched an S, so they called him Sam ever after.

Audrey had already mentioned the classic supernatural phenomena of an unexplained cold spot, but for Jane and her friend Karen it took on a more mischievous nature. Jane said that in March 2008 her friend Karen came to visit her at work while Jane was making up the rooms and cleaning the stair area. It is a straight set of stairs that splits off to two smaller sets on the left and right.

'I sat down on the steps, I could feel him, I knew he was about so I started talking to him, and all of sudden this cold air started swirling around me – so I called my friend and she sat on the other set of stairs and all of sudden he went swirling around her as well – it was just a continuous swirl of cold air around me and Karen.'

However, on another occasion earlier in 2008, Jane was going down those same stairs with a pile of dirty linen for washing and she felt a solid push from behind, so hard that she just managed to grab the handrail and save herself. Of course no one was there, just cold air. 'Thanks a lot Sam, that's really nice of you,' she thought.

She then told me how he disappeared for a few weeks and then Audrey, who had been in agony at work with a back injury, was crying with the pain when she was by herself downstairs. Jane was working upstairs and suddenly there was Sam again in front of her. Jane can't explain it but his words were inside her head as he looked at her and he said, 'Tell Audrey I don't like her crying.' Jane went to see Audrey, unaware of her tears, to take Sam's message.

On occasions when Jane enters a certain bedroom associated with Sam's appearance, there is an overwhelming smell of old-fashioned tobacco smoke, yet no one has been there to break the rules – except one person. But I suppose the 21st-century warning 'smoking kills' is rather redundant in Sam's case.

Like the Ivy House, the 14th-century Greyhound Inn in the picturesque village of Chalfont St Peter has a long and important history as a busy and bustling coaching inn. The notorious 'hanging judge' George Jeffreys is said to have held his court in a room upstairs above the main public bar. A room in which despondency, outcries of despair and the incredibly severe sentences of being hung, drawn and quartered were meted out as if his own reputation depended on proving he was the bloodiest, harshest member of the judiciary ever to have headed an English assize court. In this regard, he proved it beyond doubt.

It is also claimed that the last man to be hung for sheep stealing in the county was executed in the grounds of the pub itself.

What is so interesting about the supernatural stories that have been told about this inn over the years is the sheer evil, oppressive nature of the bloody apparitions, and the mental terror that is felt when in the room said to be have been used by Judge Jeffreys. But these have been stories, handed down and probably prone to exaggeration and certainly beyond any recorded evidence.

I was told a contemporary story, however, that really does show that something quite extraordinarily powerful is associated with a certain room, upstairs at the Greyhound.

Once more, purely through her work with local clients, Diana Canning had another brush with the supernatural – or at least her daughter did. Back in the early 1970s Diana had a patient for chiropody treatment who was the landlady of the Greyhound Inn. She asked if Diana would make a home visit to the pub one afternoon on her way home from work in order to treat her mother. Diana was living in Chalfont St Peter at the time but explained that it would be difficult because she had to pick her 6-year-old daughter up from the Holy Cross Convent and then had to get her home for a meal and homework. The landlady suggested that Diana could bring her daughter with her, she'd give her a drink and she could start her homework upstairs at the pub. Diana agreed and they both called at the Greyhound Inn as arranged after school.

They went upstairs and whilst the landlady settled Diana's daughter on a sofa outside one of the rooms, Diana went down the corridor to the far bedroom to see the landlady's mother. Her daughter started her work, knowing she only had to knock on the bedroom door if she wanted her mum.

Diana wasn't gone long but when she came out she saw her daughter anxiously waiting for her, looking ill, very pale, trembling and upset. She hadn't wanted to disturb her mother by knocking on the door. Diana asked what on earth had troubled her, what was wrong?

Diana thought she must be hungry and tired and wanted to get home. She said to her mum, 'I don't ever want to come here again, mummy.' Fighting back the tears, she said how everything went very cold and she felt someone near her, crouching over her, while something that felt like an animal, a dog maybe, was moving around her legs – but there was no one about and certainly no pet dog in the corridor. When Diana saw the landlady and told her about her daughter's distress outside room number 1, she said how sorry she was and that it was entirely her fault for being so thoughtless. She explained that people actually pay to come and stay in this particular room as it was haunted but during the night they leave as they cannot stand the terribly oppressive atmosphere and the extreme cold and things moving around them. The pub dog refused to enter the room and would disappear and hide rather than go in.

Diana's daughter had not been inside the room, and it was only late afternoon, but the malevolent presence was so strong that merely sitting outside left her young receptive mind vulnerable to its supernatural power.

The pub has recently been totally refurbished. Around 4 years ago, Diana, her husband and grandchildren were out shopping in the village. They passed the Greyhound Inn, busy with workmen as the careful process of refitting an historic building progressed. Diana's husband, who is very interested in ancient building preservation work, stopped to speak to the contractors, whilst Diana continued with the grandchildren.

When he caught up with them, he said he'd been told that two of the men on site had left – just walked away from the job never to return after their experiences working on the first floor. 'You know it's haunted on that first floor?' the contractor had told him.

'I've heard it said,' replied Diana's husband, 'I've heard it said.'

6

Atmospheric Olney and a Supernatural Legacy

THERE is something very atmospheric about Olney. Before you learn its history, traditions and folklore, a sense of profound significance pervades this bustling market town. Its proximity to Milton Keynes – proud to be new – reinforces Olney's obvious pride in antiquity and a distinct cultural heritage.

Yes, it has the Buckinghamshire legacy of being a significant lace-making centre since the 16th century when Flemish Protestants settled in the town. They were highly skilled, hard working but in dire poverty as they struggled to earn money. But Olney's lace-makers were connected with another culturally significant period of 18th-century local history when the powerful partnership of John Newton's fifteen-year preaching ministry and his hymn *Amazing Grace* dove-tailed into the profundity of William Cowper's poetry and stark observations of the town's poverty, especially amongst the lace-making community. In 1780 Cowper wrote, 'I am an Eyewitness of their poverty and do know that hundreds of this little town are upon the point of starving and that the most unremitting industry is but barely sufficient to keep them from it. There are nearly 1,200 lace makers in this beggarly town.'

'Beggarly town' is not entirely fair. It was more a town of contrasts with families of wealth and high social standing clearly evident in its local governance, patronage and industry but it did have a concentration of dreadful poverty. So it was that this small north-Buckinghamshire market town, based around the manufacture of straw plait and pillow lace-making, became a focal point for a religious fervour and a creative chemistry that was quite extraordinary.

Cowper's observation that 'variety's the very spice of life, that gives it all its flavour' has a distinct ambiguity to it where Olney is concerned, for it is here, it is claimed, the Devil himself took up residence, favouring the earthly pleasures of this Buckinghamshire town, 'dancing in empty pockets'.

So you will see, before any supernatural stories are teased out from the nooks and crannies of this highly atmospheric 21st-century location, it already lays claim to the ultimate supernatural town resident – the Devil.

I was taken by Lewis Kitchener, author of *The Heart and Soul of Olney*, to visit the Whirly Pit at the north end of town. On a pleasant March day, we stared into the depths of the pond's dark waters and I could believe that this was, as claimed, a bottomless pit fed by an undetected, mysterious spring – a pond that can never dry up.

Lewis explained that in a time long past at an unknown date – along the Warrington Road toward Olney came the Devil in a chariot, his headless coachmen matched by a team of headless horses. It was a night of the darkest hue and midnight was approaching.

At tremendous speed, the coach plunged into the Whirly Pit, dropping down to a cavernous passage that took the ultimate purveyor of evil to a place known as Goosey Bridge. At this point the coach burst above ground once more into Sway Gog meadow, blasting its turfs and soil high into the air as it journeyed on at breakneck speed to its unknown destination.

Today, this story has two legacies. One claims that as midnight approaches, at unpredictable times of the year, the sound of the Devil's coach and horses can still be heard approaching and plunging into the Whirly Pit. The other is that if you are in the vicinity of Weston where the Sway Gog is still to be found, you will feel vibrations like those of an impending earthquake.

Finding a contemporary witness to either of these events has not proved possible but what Oliver Ratcliff referred to as 'Olney Devil

Lore' in his 1907 Almanac, is very clear about the Devil having taken up residence in the town, clear enough to pinpoint the exact area of the High Street where historic cottages are still located. The Devil made appearances to those who chose to see him, particularly in the Two Brewers pub in the High Street, still a bustling business today.

It became the Devil's local pub and he caused nothing but trouble for the landlord who had to dance, jig and run to the Devil's bidding, ignoring his more earthly patrons who became fearful of the Devil's presence and began to take their custom elsewhere.

Ratcliff wryly observes, 'His patrons were getting fewer and fewer, and they would instinctively shrink from coming into contact with the Devil, though at the same time they might be constant worshippers at his shrine.'

It took 13 priests, complete with bell, book and candle to challenge him, and one priest in particular to outwit him. When the Devil refused the priests' demands that he should refrain from his visits for 100 years, the quick-thinking priest asked, 'Will you postpone your visits until this candle I hold in my hand is burnt out?'

The Devil agreed, and as Ratcliff explains, 'thereupon the priest blew out the candle and placed it at the bottom of a well in the yard. If the re-lighting of this candle is to bring about a renewal of these visits, it is hoped in the interests of all concerned, that no meddling busybody will succeed in identifying this well and bringing the candle to light.'

So that is where the Devil and Olney apparently parted company – but with a hidden well and a ceremonial candle still unaccounted for, anything is possible.

An ancient Olney building in Market Square was being renovated recently when one of the builders discovered a very old child's shoe secreted in the chimney area. Rather than throw it away, he decided to keep it and took it home. From that moment onwards he experienced nothing but bad luck and a series of unfortunate events.

Lewis Kitchener told me, 'He had an accident, his wife left him, and he developed an incurable illness, and he put it all down to possession of the shoe.' Lewis also confided that the apparition of a young girl had been seen wandering in that building. People also reported that there was the sound of a young girl crying when the shoe went missing. The atmosphere of restlessness continued until the shoe was returned. It now has pride of place, encapsulated in a glass box incorporated into the building work of the back stair wall.

Why the shoe? Could there be a powerful force connected with the concealment of such an innocent object? Certainly, there could, given the early Olney claim of its association with the Devil. Already deeply embedded in Buckinghamshire folklore was the story associated with Sir John Schorne, rector of North Marston about 24 miles from Olney, who, it was claimed, 'conjured the Devil into a boot'.

Boots and shoes, particularly children's shoes, became a form of insurance against evil spirits invading your home. One of the most vulnerable parts of the home is the hearth, which is open to the sky, so a child's shoe hidden on a ledge inside the hearth would, it was believed, provide protection from the supernatural. The protection ceases as soon as the shoe is taken away from the building and bad luck follows. This was certainly the case for the Olney builder.

June Swann from the Northampton Museum has made a study of shoes concealed in buildings and says that when she first started her work in the 1950s the shoes 'had come mostly from chimneys, and I recall being particularly puzzled by a small pair of child's boots found in the thatch of a cottage in Stanwick, Northamptonshire and wondered what sort of people allowed a child so small to lose its boots on the roof.' (Swan, J., *Shoes Concealed in Buildings*, Costume No. 30 1996)

Of course now the supernatural significance has been well documented by June who has since gathered evidence from people who did allow the shoes to leave the house. They would experience strange noises of distress and small tremors in the house. She recalls one case where the boots that had been found were sent to an exhibition. While the boots were gone, the home owners had an extraordinary run of bad luck including flooding, the death of their pets and a collapsed outhouse. The boots are now safely back and are not to be touched.

Intrigued, I visited the location in Market Square only to find it was empty awaiting new tenants – apparently a tea shop was to open there soon. For as long as the locals can remember this has been a shop or commercial premises of one kind of another. Lewis told me it was originally a bakehouse, where people used to take their meats to the oven for roasting.

In later years it became famous as Mrs Loom's café – renowned for her jam doughnuts made especially for every market day, apparently an indulgence so sumptuous you could understand the Devil's interest in Olney.

It has also done service as a Chinese restaurant. Its last incarnation, however, was as The Flower Shop now moved across the Square. Without warning, I turned up at the re-located flower shop to ask about working life in the old shop premises and discovered Barbara Harvey busy at work arranging a bouquet. 'We did use to have a few little odd things happening,' she told me. 'I personally, and I know quite a few of my colleagues, felt someone touch their hair as we walked down the shop.'

This was interesting, one of the key signs of supernatural activity can often be a light touching of the head – could it be the little girl whose shoe was hidden in the hearth? But the story had a twist to it. Very often Barbara would sense somebody standing close to her, smoking. The smell of cigarette smoke was very strong, she said, yet her working companion across the bench would sense and smell nothing. Then another time the situation would reverse, Barbara would smell nothing but her companion would. That rules out the little girl, so who was touching heads and smoking and was it not frightening?

'I know it's an odd thing to say,' replied Barbara, 'but you get used to it. Momentarily you think, ooh what was that? Before we moved in, there was some work going on, to accommodate us, and there were offices upstairs. I believe that somebody brought their son or daughter in who saw an old man on the staircase and asked "Who is that old man?" We never saw an old man, however.'

'But it could have been him smoking?' I suggested.

'Could have been,' said Barbara.

When investigating supernatural stories, it helps when others have witnessed or experienced the same phenomena. With my unannounced visit and discussion with Barbara finished, her colleague Kirsty arrived back from lunch-break totally unaware of who I was or the details of our conversation. So I asked her about her time in the old premises across the square. Kirsty told me that she had worked in the very old alley which connected the front of the shop with a newer workroom at the back.

'Twice I've felt somebody put their hand on my shoulder – hard enough for me to know somebody is there and to turn around. It was a lot of pressure – a very hard pressure – a distinct hand pressure, but there was never anyone there when I turned around. I didn't feel scared though!'

She told me about a girl who worked there at the computer and several times she reporting seeing a man with an old cap in the alley.

She also recalled the smell of cigarette smoke – it even made her cough but there was no one smoking there. She confirmed that each would experience the smell one at a time, never together.

Kirsty also recalled that the shop owner's daughter had called by when the premises were being refurbished for the flower shop and would keep asking, 'What's that man doing?' But nobody else could see a man.

Kirsty, now reminded of these events, was deep in thought and, as if she needed to re-affirm her very real experiences, added, 'I know I was not imagining it. It was a proper hand, so obvious. It happened twice in the same little alleyway.'

'That's where I had someone touch my hair!' exclaimed Barbara as if comparing experiences for the first time.

I left them reminiscing about their encounters with the

unexplained, while I made a mental note to visit a certain tea shop in the near future – the devil I will!

Before we leave Olney, we must pay heed to the White Lady of High Street North. This is a very particular lady who has been seen by the occasional Olney resident but only at times of renovation, refurbishment and rebuilding. It is somewhat of a mystery that she is called the White Lady as she is always seen dressed in black from head to toe. Her reason for appearing when building work is in progress appears to be one of architectural taste, judging by some recent episodes in the High Street.

To quote from Lewis Kitchener, 'By all accounts she likes to inspect the work, making sure that it comes up to standard. Woe betide you if you take a short-cut, or do something wrong, she will soon let you know about it.'

Well, apparently she did not like the appearance and convenience-food style of the new One-Stop shop being built to replace a traditional grocery store in the High Street very recently.

Also when the previous owners moved out they took a collection of gravestones with them. There were quite a few around the garden when they moved in and they wanted to take them to their new garden now they had retired. A spooky kind of souvenir.

The builders moved in, totally unaware that burials appeared to have taken place on that site. They were also only familiar with the local council inspection requirements for their work – not that of the White Lady of High Street North. Lewis recalls, 'They did this work and nothing went right for these builders. Nothing whatsoever. It turned out to be the job from hell.'

They struggled towards opening day with snags and delays and malfunctioning equipment but this was just the lead-up to the climax of the White Lady's disapproval. The evening before the grand opening, the brand new, state-of the-art boiler exploded. Down came the ceiling amid a flood that ensured any customers would be wading through two inches of water with more on the way.

The builders had to hastily drill holes through the laminate floor to release the water.

The builder in charge said at the time he has never been on such a cursed job – nothing went right for them and it is still not going right for them now they have finished.

Was it the removal of the gravestones that caused the unrest, or the disapproval of the White Lady of High Street North? Perhaps a combination of the two.

I also suspect that the builder preferred the supernatural explanation for all the building disasters to one of mere earthly dimensions. The job from hell it may have turned out to be but for the future it is wise to recall an old Irish proverb. 'The Devil never grants long leases.'

Olney may well be in line for some more surprises to come.

7

Ghostly Goings On in the Swan Theatre

YOUNG Tom Schoon had been working under the watchful eye of the senior stage door keeper, Bob Eastland, at the Wycombe Swan Theatre for some months and Bob was pleased with his progress.

Bob had worked as door keeper since 1998, after 23 years as a fireman. Now, in 2006, he was keen for Tom to learn the ropes as thoroughly as possible.

One of the most important jobs was the 'lock-up' – to make sure that the theatre buildings and certain rooms and facilities were securely locked up for the night once all the staff had left.

Security for actors, staff and visitors, as well as valuable props, personal possessions and expensive technical equipment was paramount. Once the show or rehearsal was over, and everyone had left the building and the paperwork was complete, lock-up could begin.

Opened in 1992, the Swan is a modern theatre, but alongside it is the Oak Room, belonging to the old town hall, which dates from 1903 and forms part of the theatre complex – a successful mixture of old and new. The responsibility for the security of all of this was Bob's, and he took the role very seriously indeed.

This particular evening in 2006, Bob decided Tom had learnt the lock-up round thoroughly enough to do it alone, while he kept in radio contact at the stage door office.

Tom set off. The first part of the route was a little scary as the Tudor Rooms across the road from the theatre are rumoured to be haunted. Bob assured Tom that he had never seen a ghost there but it was true that his predecessor had claimed there was a woman in Tudor clothes who strolled between the pillars in the Oak Room. He had told Bob, 'It's quite all right, she's very friendly, doesn't do you any harm, just wish her "good evening" and pass on by.'

Bob guessed he might have been kidding him as he was the 'new boy' at the time, but, just in case, he did have his own lock-up ritual. On the way down the sweeping staircase is a marble bust of a woman. 'Evening,' Bob would say every time he went past – just in case. It pays to keep on the good side of a ghost.

Tom was making his rounds in the town hall and was feeling a little spooked as it is eerie with its underground passages and robing rooms. Underground passages at night are not somewhere to be alone in the dark when there are rumours of ghosts. Relieved to have completed that side of the lock-up, it was good to get back to the modern corridors of the Swan.

Meanwhile, Bob, back at the stage door, knew Tom was competent at lock-up; he'd proved himself by now so Bob thought he'd help him out so they could get away on time.

'I knew he could lock up the band pit and the area downstairs quite adequately so I thought I'd save him a couple of minutes, I'd radio and go and do it. I went down there, turned all the lights off, locked all the doors, everything else, came back to the stage door office and radioed him and said, "Tom, you don't need to go down to the band pit because I've turned all the lights off and locked everything up – all done." '

Tom replied, 'What do you mean it's all done?'

Bob explained again that he had been down there, locked all the doors and put out the lights to save a bit of time. Tom said that he couldn't have done, all the lights were on and all the doors unlocked. He was, at that moment, putting out the lights and locking the doors.

Bob couldn't believe it, 'Come on!' he said, 'I've been down there and done it already.' Bob knew that in the time available, Tom could not have gone round and turned all the lights on and undone all the doors as a 'wind-up' and anyway Tom was not that sort of person. They both wanted to get home and Bob doing that part of the lock-up would save them both time.

Bob and Tom both admit to being quite unnerved by this experience and were genuinely shaken. There was absolutely no natural explanation why locked doors and extinguished lights suddenly became unlocked with lights blazing when Tom arrived.

Bob took me on the same lock-up route. The concrete passageway under the stage and out to the other side is quite eerie, albeit modern. The engineering secrets of stage trapdoors, and other mechanical devices loom into view, silently waiting to come to life.

You enter one door and lock it behind you, turn off the lights, exit through another door, and lock it behind you with a decisive clunk, and so on, in a circular pattern until you arrive back at the stage door. You cannot imagine that you have done this – you know you have done it.

It is a clear, precise action yet somehow, on that night, with two witnesses, those same doors became unlocked and the lights were switched back on while only Tom and Bob were in the building. But were they?

There is another incident which Bob revealed but whether there is any connection between the two is unclear. About six months after he had started as assistant stage door manager in 1998, there were rumours of hauntings in the theatre but Bob was not someone to believe in such things. Like Tom, he was entrusted with the lock-up and crossed the dark auditorium which was lit only by the aptly named 'ghost lights' that just give enough illumination for the cleaners to do their job, other areas are pitch black.

It was about 11 pm as Bob was crossing the circle area of the theatre. About halfway across, he stopped in his tracks. Someone was sitting on a seat directly in front of him. Bob knew he was the only person in the building. The technicians were in the Hobgoblin pub having a drink with a colleague who was leaving, and Bob was going over to join them after the lock-up.

Bob recalls, 'I noticed this person sitting on the seat directly in front of me in the circle seats. I thought this is strange because there is no one else in the building except myself. He just looked like an ordinary person sitting there wearing an anorak type jacket. I said, "Oh excuse me, can I help you? What are you doing here?" As I got closer, he just vanished and there was just an empty chair.'

Bob is clear it was not a trick of the light – there was someone sitting in the seat and he melted away as he questioned and approached him. Feeling a bit shaken, he finished locking up and went to the Hobgoblin pub.

'You'll never guess what I've just seen,' he told his colleagues. But before he could say any more one of the technicians stopped him and whispered something to Bobby Pie whose leaving party it was, then he asked Bob to continue.

Bob told them what had happened. Bobby Pie turned to the others with amazement. That was just what his colleague had whispered to him. This was the 'haunting' referred to when Bob started working there. No one had told him the details and the technician had never revealed his story before – but they matched exactly.

The origin of this supernatural event is a challenge to pinpoint. Some clues as to 'haunting connections' with the Swan were revealed in 2006 when the famous Irish medium Sharon Neill was booked to give a show there. She is famous for being the UK's only blind medium.

Blind from birth, she was only 5 years old when she realised that 'people' spoke to her when she was in bed at night. This was very frightening at the time for the little girl but later she came to realise she could communicate with dead people and that they were trying to attract her attention, before she was old enough to understand what was happening. Now in her forties, she claims that eight such deceased people are now constantly with her as her guides. She told the *Psychic Times*, 'I cannot explain it. I don't think anyone could … it's beyond explanation.'

Being blind she cannot be accused, as other mediums sometimes are, of picking up cues and clues through body language. As she has never been able to see, it is uncanny that she can describe the appearance of somebody who has died or point to a location on a map she cannot see.

When her grandmother died she began to visit Sharon who, for the first time, was able to 'see' her and describe her exactly to her mother, who was dumbfounded by the accuracy. Now she has become one of a growing band of celebrity mediums and the Wycombe Swan hosted part of her 2006 tour.

Accompanied by Liz Stanley, the Swan Theatre's press officer at the time, Sharon was taken to the Oak Room entrance. She immediately felt a marked drop in temperature. As she ventured further towards the two central pillars that Bob Eastland had been told marked the spot haunted by a lady in Tudor costume, Sharon stopped and spoke, not about such a lady but two other 'spirits'.

'There is activity all around me,' she said. 'I have a gentleman standing in front of me. He'd be around 5 ft 6 ins or 5 ft 7 ins, maybe in his late 40s or 50s. He's dressed in a proper suit, double-breasted, with a white shirt. There's actually two people here. There's a domestic woman. She's smaller than him and has an apron on. Her hair is tied back in a little hat or a cap or something, in a bun.'

After a short silence, Sharon then laughed, saying, 'She's just asked me if I want anything to drink, but the man is quite cross and has asked me why I am here. He disapproves of the way the building is being used now.' (*Bucks Free Press*, 14 February 2006.)

Is this man Bob and Tom's 'ghost', playing tricks unlocking locked doors and putting on lights because he is cross the theatre now uses the historic Oak Room for murder-mystery events and other theatrical entertainments?

I spoke with Sharon about her visit to the Oak Room and she recalls it very vividly indeed. She feels most certainly that this man had something to do with important legal activities in that location but he died suddenly from a heart-attack.

Although dead, his spirit thinks he is alive and is angry about being ignored. What better way to be noticed than to interfere with the locking up of the theatre – except he's only done it once, if indeed it was him!

During her 2006 visit Sharon thought his name could be Woolham or Warham – she accused him of mumbling, but she had been certain it began with a W and ended with an M and is etched on a copper plaque somewhere in the room. Was it perhaps William? There are several eminent 'Williams' on the memorial plaque of a former mayor as well as etched on the stained-glass windows. When we spoke recently two years on from this experience, she told me that, thinking about it later, he was definitely saying William. What was so remarkable about this information is that Sharon would have absolutely no idea that there was a stained-glass window with the name William etched into it, yet there was.

So is the Swan haunted? It seems clear from several independent experiences that some supernatural activity does characterise not only the old Oak Room, but has made its presence known in the new theatre. In centuries to come, will the 'Old Wycombe Swan' become a supernatural tale in a book, not dissimilar to this? You never know – all ghosts have to start somewhere.

8

The Ellesborough Happening

W HEN the well-known children's author Alison Uttley was asked to write about Buckinghamshire, she did so with a passion. She said, 'This county of Buckinghamshire is the epitome of England, and the way of living is that of country people, and I have fallen in love with its beauty and changelessness.' (Uttley, A., *Buckinghamshire*, 1950)

Nearly sixty years later a great deal has changed of course, but her description of Ellesborough's church remains true. 'There is something stark and grand about its outline against the sky,' she said, and indeed there is. When she approached the church all those years ago from the Aylesbury road, she conjured up a quite remarkable image. From afar, she likened the view to '… a stone ship, riding a green sea, poised on a curving green wave in the distance', and she saw it also as 'a place of extraordinary life'. She was aware that this fine church had long been thought haunted but found this to be of no particular surprise, commenting, 'One can well imagine men coming back to that resting place under the Chilterns. Beacon Hill is behind it, towering over it and on a shoulder of Beacon Hill is Cymbeline's Mount.'

So is there evidence to support the return of departed souls to this 'resting place under the Chilterns'?

At the time of Uttley's visit the vicar was clearly keen to emphasise that they were standing on the Icknield Way, thought to be the oldest road in Britain. Such a prehistoric pathway would have seen many lives come and go, but are some such ancient travellers still to be encountered today? The answer appears to be yes.

Certainly there are records up to the 1970s of a figure in medieval costume walking slowly across the nave towards the far wall of the church. He was first seen in the 1940s by the church organist a few years before Alison Uttley's visit. The organist was practising for a Sunday service when he noticed the heavy church door opening and shutting, and then saw an extremely tall man dressed in 14th-century clothing walk slowly through the church. The man disappeared behind a corner pillar and failed to re-emerge. When the organist investigated, there was absolutely no one there. This pattern continued at times when there was only one person in the church. Certainly up to the 1970s reports of sightings were still being made.

Another incident in the 1970s, in the time of the late Revd Norman White, was the appearance to parishioners of a young woman dressed in white, walking ceremoniously through the church to disappear near a door at the southern end. The Reverend himself spoke of how he saw her moving slowly away from the altar steps before fading from view. There was a theory that she was a parishioner in love with Robert Wallis, rector of the church in the 17th century, but the origin of this story is now lost in time. When I spoke with local historian John Vince, who knew Norman White very well, about this sighting of which he had spoken quite openly, John was clear on one thing. 'If Norman said he saw it then he saw it – he was a very rational, objective man,' said Mr Vince firmly.

I was fortunate to speak with the Revd David Horner who was Norman White's successor. What he told me confirmed that there was something supernatural associated with the church – an apparition – possibly of a woman but in black rather than white. He knows because he experienced it outside the church in the early 1980s. This is the Revd David Horner's story as told to me.

'On a pleasant summer evening in 1980, I set off from the rectory to take evening service at the church of St Peter and St Paul, the parish church of Ellesborough. The rectory was only a couple of hundred yards from the church but the latter half of the walk was up a steep footpath, the church being on the top of a small hill.

'I had just got to the steep bit when I saw in front of me – about 30 yards in front – a person dressed in a longish black coat also walking up the path. From the appearance of the person from behind I thought it was a lady who was always in good time for the service and who sang in the choir, known to everybody as 'Auntie Nellie'. I thought I'd try and catch up with her to greet her but then the unexpected happened. I was within 4 or 5 yards behind when the person simply vanished.'

David was astounded – this happened on an open pathway on a clear summer's evening right in front of his eyes – she just disappeared.

'I can remember it today as clearly as I saw it on that evening so long ago,' he told me. But his story doesn't end there. 'About a week later, my son Stephen said to me, "Dad, you won't believe what I've just seen up the path to the church." "I bet I will," I answered.'

Stephen had seen what appeared to be a figure in a cloak on the same path who also faded from sight. Until they swapped stories they did not know of each other's separate encounter, but as David confirmed to me, 'He had seen the same as I had.'

David has thought long and hard about this experience ever since and wonders if it is connected with a local story he was told about the ghost of a clergyman who had supposedly committed suicide there. He feels what he and Stephen saw in Ellesborough was clearly 'the picture of a "happening", which was a happening involving an extremely strong emotion, such as immediately before and leading to a suicide. I believe that such an emotion can create an imprint on the atmosphere around where that emotion happened and that emotion can invade the mind or spirit of some people who are receptive to this sort of thing.'

David is right in that there is no doubt that 'sensitives' do exist who claim to be able to tune into past events that have such strong emotional ingredients. David and Stephen certainly qualify, perhaps you do too. Now you have a chance to find out, if you visit a certain church at Ellesborough on a summer's eve.

9

Halton House's Special Party Guests

B UILDING a magnificent French-style chateau with beautifully landscaped gardens in the Buckinghamshire countryside for lavish entertaining and sumptuous parties is not within the means or ambitions of most people. But for Alfred de Rothschild it most certainly was.

Halton Mansion, completed in 1883 after only three years of building, was ahead of its time, being fully supplied with both gas and electricity, boasting effective under-floor heating, and even a forerunner to the modern sauna. Its 18th-century French furniture, old masters and fine porcelain gave rise to the expression 'Le Style Rothschild'.

Today, it is part of RAF Halton, and is called simply Halton House. It looks as magnificent as ever. Its impressive chateau-style exterior, lakes and gardens and amazing interiors have become a favourite choice for many feature films and television serials. Its bustle and business is to provide accommodation for RAF Halton officers as well as conference facilities.

It seems, however, that there are still some guests left behind from the glories of those early party days, unaware that the party's over and the carriages left more than 100 years ago. Take the gentleman in the black top hat, dressed for dinner in his jacket and tails, who will regularly stroll through what used to be Alfred's dining room to fade away through the window at the far end. These days, it is a bar and function room rather than a dining room so he's affectionately known as 'the gentleman in the bar'.

In following up this reported apparition, I was fortunate to visit Halton House with Squadron Leader Colin Baker who is RAF Halton's resident historian. He explained that this was a gentleman, whose name is not known, who came to one of Alfred's parties with his fiancée but she 'two-timed' him by leaving the party with another man. It is thought his emotions ran so high, and so distraught was he, that he still returns today to search for his lost love.

New staff members, unaware of the story, will sometimes ask about him. The last reported sighting was early in 2008.

Sqn Ldr Baker explained, 'The last person to actually see him said that he has got green lapels on his black jacket – when they looked at each other they jumped back in amazement and when the woman went to look again he had actually disappeared so it seems it was the ghost that was scared away.'

The woman who saw him said it really frightened her – it was such a surprise when she realised he was in fact a ghost. Sqn Ldr Baker describes him as around 5 ft 9 ins tall and wearing a black jacket with tails and green lapels. He is definitely dressed for dinner, but his age is difficult to determine.

Now all that remains is to find out who he is, but that might never be known. Perhaps he has a connection with the Graceful Lady?

This Halton House spectre has been reported by many visitors and officers. The lady, in full Victorian dress, is seen either coming down the flowing curved stairs into that same dining room, or hurrying up the stairs to disappear into one of the rooms.

Sqn Ldr Baker told me, 'Quite a few people have seen a lady come from the left side, in Victorian attire with a splendid hat – she actually comes down the stairs and turns into the bar. Now, we are not sure whether the two are related, but she's dressed in all her splendour, a huge ball gown with a sort of tassel at the back.'

The 'gentleman in the bar' and now 'the graceful lady', both way out of time and reluctant to leave what was then Halton Mansion. Others who are reluctant to leave have only been heard, not seen.

This third story is one the most interesting supernatural puzzles I have encountered.

Upstairs we visited the snooker room which immediately strikes you as being unusually cold, particularly given its prominent location overlooking the gardens on what was a sunny day. Sqn Ldr Baker said it always has a cold atmosphere, this was normal, but what is not normal is the ghostly game of snooker that is played there.

Right alongside this room is one of the bedrooms used by officers staying at Halton House. As this is what is known as a transitional officers' mess lots of personnel are passing through, staying one night or more and moving on. So it is very interesting that many complaints are received from the diverse occupants of that nearby bedroom about sounds of laughter and billiard balls clicking together as a game of snooker is in progress around 2 am. Being woken by snooker players is one thing, but going to the room itself, literally seconds away from the bedroom door, and finding it silent, in darkness with an unfinished game of snooker on the table is quite another.

The assumption that mistakes might have been made does not explain the high numbers of reports that have been received. Sqn Ldr Baker was prepared to accept that some people might have dreamt about playing snooker after seeing the room next door. Others might have actually played a game and in their dream think they still are, and wake up. That might account for one or two reports, but not the eight or so reported, the last one being just at the end of 2007.

'There are things that are going on which are unexplainable. Just goes to show that spirits and ghosts do have a bit of fun occasionally,' he added.

Also, in recent years, one part of the accommodation area has become a no-go area for dogs and it is not the residents who are enforcing the ban. Their pet dogs refuse to walk down a particular section of corridor when being taken out for a walk. The frustrated owners now have to walk around the longest route possible to the

70

outside to avoid this more convenient exit shunned by the sensitive canines who simply will not budge, but will happily turn around and scoot off in the other direction.

The final supernatural story is very sad and concerns a Chinese laundry worker who worked for Alfred Charles Rothschild for over 20 years. When Rothschild died on 1 January 1918 this loyal servant fell into a deep depression.

'When Alfred died,' explained Sqn Ldr Baker, 'he knew that Lionel Nathan de Rothschild, Alfred's nephew, was not going to reside here and he would lose his job, which immediately put him into a state of sadness and distress. He decided to take his life. He walked right up to the top of the lift shaft, some 80 ft high, and hung himself. Since then many people have either heard or seen him carrying out his duties – only momentarily – but a definite glimpse.'

'Also,' confided Colin, 'it is not uncommon for both staff and the officers who actually stay here to say they get a very uneasy feeling about this particular area of the stairway.'

Maybe the dogs have picked up on this too and sense what may lie ahead if they are taken too far in that direction.

So while two distinguished guests still seek to stay at the party, and others, yet unseen, enjoy their late game of snooker, and the dogs devise their own exit policy from the house, the loyal servant tries to retain his attachment to the work he so diligently carried out over all those years for his employer Alfred Charles Rothschild. He too wished to stay and, seemingly, he has done just that.

10

Woodrow High House and the Green Lady

Tucked away in the Buckinghamshire countryside is a very special country house. Providing the most amazing adventures for around 5,000 young people every year, Woodrow High House is owned by the Federation of London Youth Clubs and in their words, 'provides a kaleidoscope of training and activity opportunities ... a journey to opportunity and discovery.'

Aimed predominantly at inner-city youngsters, it takes them into the countryside to assist with their personal development, teach them new skills and take them on new adventures. For one city lad it was more than an adventure – it was a journey into the realm of the supernatural – one he will never forget.

Woodrow High House was presented to the London Federation of Boys' Clubs as a training centre by the Goldsmiths' Company in 1946. It was formally opened by the Permanent Secretary to the Ministry of Education, John Maud. However, it needed a lot of work and cleaning up so the early groups of young lads from London were brought down for long weekends to help get it into shape. One particular weekend in September was to prove quite extraordinary.

Terry Lawson was the appointed 'Secretary for Training'. He arrived at the house with a lorry load of furniture and fittings on a Friday afternoon, ahead of the youngsters who were due the next day to help him sort it all out.

As the autumn evening drew in, this enormous mansion took on a whole new atmosphere. Large, empty, dusty rooms lit only by candlelight produced strange shadows and shapes where the white dust sheets lay ghost-like over dining room chairs. Electricity was still a distant luxury but how Terry wished he could just turn on a switch and see what lay ahead in the dark corners and twisting stairways. Walking alone through these vast rooms, his candle flickering furiously in the wind blowing through broken windowpanes, was not a pleasant experience. The sound of an owl hooting and the screaming bark of foxes echoed in the distant woods.

Suddenly he stopped as the candlelight revealed a pale face with dark penetrating eyes and short dark hair. Ahead on the wall was a portrait of a woman wearing a striking green dress – his first introduction to the Green Lady. This was the picture of Lady Helena Stanhope who lived in Woodrow High House in the late 17th century.

He stared, and she appeared to stare back – her dark eyes piercing the room despite the poor light.

Terry quickly hurried upstairs. He had taken a small bedroom in the oldest wing of the house and was so tired he soon fell asleep but later he awoke with a start.

It was pitch black. He had no idea of the time. He sat still and listened. His heart pounded as he heard footsteps in the passage outside his room – a regular, echoing footfall.

But there was another sound, a swishing noise like a gentle wave or rustling leaves, followed by a slight dragging echo. He managed to light a candle and cautiously, nervously, opened the bedroom door to peer outside into the corridor.

Eerie silence. Nothing to be seen nor heard.

He closed the door and went back to bed but was woken again by the sound of a clock striking three downstairs although his watch showed it was only just after midnight. Once more he heard the footsteps and the rustling, dragging sound. And it was coming right up to his door. He waited. The footsteps continued and went into another room. He heard the door open and close. Not feeling brave enough to venture out again, he wedged a chair under the door handle and decided to sit out the night, but did eventually fall into a deep sleep.

The next morning a tired Terry Lawson greeted an excited party of lads from London as they began their countryside adventure at Woodrow High House.

Terry managed to make all the hard work in clearing and cleaning the house good fun, encouraging them to find secret panels and passages, and to explore the large gardens and out-houses. It really was a wonderful contrast to the pavements and tarmac of London. After a long, exciting day, the lads had tea and went to bed tired.

One boy in particular, Jack from the Crown and Manor Club in Hoxton, decided to have his own adventure and look for secret passages downstairs. Putting his jacket over his pyjamas, and slipping on his wellington boots, he crept out of the makeshift dormitory along the passage to the stairs.

Just as he started down the stairs he heard footsteps behind him and realised he had been found out. But when he turned around it wasn't Terry coming to fetch him back. Heading straight towards him was a dark-haired lady with an anxious, worried face, her piercing eyes looking straight through him.

He pressed against the wall and she hurried past him and down the stairs – her green dress swishing and dragging along the floor.

Too much had now happened to go back to bed, the others wouldn't believe him anyway – this was an adventure and he decided to follow her.

She had hurried into the dining room heading straight for the window and seemed to dissolve through it. Jack found an open side door and raced around in time to see the moonlit figure go over the disused drawbridge towards the distant woods.

The sounds of the night were more frightening to Jack than his quest to follow the lady in green. He was not used to woodland noises from owls and foxes and creaking trees but he kept his composure and watched her enter the wood. He followed her as best as he could but she had disappeared.

By now he had lost his sense of direction so pushed his way through the undergrowth and stumbled into a moonlit grotto – old ivy-covered brick walls glinted and glistened with moisture. Perhaps this was the entrance to a secret passage.

He turned and raced back to the house as fast as he could. As he got back inside the house he could see a cellar door slowly opening and once more the lady came into view – she was very distraught and weeping bitterly.

As she passed the grandfather clock to rush upstairs, it chimed three times. Jack knew it could not possibly be that late, he followed behind her up the stairs and watched her struggle to keep her composure as, sobbing, she made her way along the passage where he knew Mr Lawson had his bedroom. She hesitated outside his room and then continued to the next bedroom. Jack summoned up every ounce of courage, caught her up and as she entered the room so did he, just as the door closed behind him.

She turned to face him but seemed not to see him and merely looked right through the petrified young boy and moved across the room to open a small fitted cupboard by the fireplace. She pulled from it a bottle and without hesitation, drank from it. Her face, already distraught with grief, was now twisted in agony as she collapsed on the floor in front of the terrified lad and vanished.

Jack wrenched open the door and ran as fast as possible to the dormitory room, clattering in to wake all the others. Jack was quite deeply affected by what he had experienced and, for his own sake, Terry arranged for him to go home that morning.

Some days later, when Jack had calmed down, Terry spent some time with him in London, writing down his story as accurately as possible. Terry, of course, had no reason to doubt what Jack had told him as he had personally experienced the footsteps leaving the house, the chiming clock and the footsteps passing his room, but he had not been as brave as Jack who investigated further.

Once Jack's story of the Green Lady was told it was researched to see if it had any basis in reality. What had happened at Woodrow

High House all those years ago to produce such a spectacular apparition and supernatural adventure?

Today's director of Woodrow High House, Roy Hickman, met me in the room where Jack saw the Green Lady disappear after apparently drinking poison from a bottle. Now known as the Cromwell Room (Oliver Cromwell and his family lived there during the Civil War) it retains a certain air of mystery, and I noticed a small cupboard door by the fireplace wall is just slightly open as if ready for the Green Lady's return visit.

Over the years a number of people have claimed to have seen the Green Lady but Roy has not yet had that privilege. He explained that documents found in the house, and local knowledge, had helped in the piecing together of the most remarkable story of Lady Helena Stanhope and Sir Peter Bostock to whom Lady Helena was betrothed.

The illegitimate son of Charles II, James Scott, 1st Duke of Monmouth, claimed he was the rightful heir to the English throne and plotted to overthrow James II. Now known as the Monmouth Rebellion (or Pitchfork Rebellion) a handful of nobles supported James Scott's cause including Sir Peter Bostock. So, against the Catholic monarchy, the Protestant supporters of Monmouth fought a battle on the bleak lowland moors of Somerset on 6 July 1685.

Despite outnumbering the royal forces, their lack of training and shortage of muskets saw them routed after only three hours. So began the Bloody Assizes of the notorious Judge Jeffreys as the rebels were tracked down and executed.

Lady Helena Stanhope was desperately waiting for news of her husband-to-be, Sir Peter Bostock, and after his precarious and dangerous journey from that Somerset battlefield, Sir Peter sought sanctuary at Woodrow High House under Lady Helena's care. However, Sir Peter was being pursued by the king's agents so she hid him in the grotto in the woods. By a tragic twist of fate, Royalist supporters saw her taking food to him, thereby giving away his hiding place. When she next went to see him she found his dead and broken body in what is today the paddock of Woodrow High House.

Distraught with grief, she ran into the house through the cellar and up to her room where she took a large draught of deadly poison, collapsing on the floor in the throes of death.

It seems that it took an adventurous young lad from Hoxton to cross into this supernatural energy force. A force of such magnitude that he was able to watch the whole sorry tale that occurred over three centuries ago. It also turned out that the place where Jack saw her apparently dissolve through a window was once the location of the original front door to the house.

Jack could have had no knowledge of this historical event and it was only because of his detailed description, told to an enterprising Terry Lawson, that we today have a glimpse into a truly spectacular supernatural adventure.

*****

Roy Hickman, the current director at Woodrow High House, had not been in his post long before he too had cause to encounter the Green Lady, but in rather different circumstances. He has not seen her ghost, nevertheless he cannot explain exactly what occurred during some remedial work for dry rot in the main house early in 1985.

The treatment experts surveyed the spread of this destructive fungus, looking in the cellar and beneath the plaster in what is now called the Assembly Room where ancient timbers are embedded in the walls. It is in this room that two portraits hang, those of Lady Helena Stanhope and Sir Peter Bostock.

When the extent of the necessary treatment had been decided, Roy was advised to remove all valuable items and furnishings from the room as they would not be covered by the builder's insurance should they get damaged and the use of chemical sprays could possibly taint the velvet drapes and other delicate items. It was early on Monday morning and the workmen were due to start so Roy set to work. Having moved the furniture and fittings he started to take down Sir Peter Bostock's portrait – but it would not budge.

He discovered that the method of hanging the heavy-framed portrait was devised to prevent any chance of accidental detachment from the wall. Two metal rods, set well into the wall, protruded out and curved upwards into brackets, requiring a matching tubular structure, fixed to the back of the portrait, to be slid down over the rods. These fixed rods in the tight tubular frames had become almost welded together over the years with grime and surface rust. The portrait would not budge.

Roy told me, 'I thought, I am going to damage something if I am not careful here – so anyway, first off I used a bit of butter then some WD40 oil – eventually after a lot of work I could get it off the wall.'

The builders arrived to start work and all that was now left was the portrait of the Green Lady, now alone in the room, parted from Sir Peter Bostock once more.

Roy recalls asking the builders, 'Is it really essential that I take this down? It's hard work and could take quite a time and I don't want to damage it.' They said, 'Well that's up to you mate, there are spores and stuff that fly around.' They put down a big polythene sheet across the middle of the room, all carefully taped to contain the spray, so Roy said 'Let's leave it.'

Roy had already seen how Lady Helena Stanhope's portrait was fixed as solidly as Sir Peter's so it was his calculated decision to leave her alone rather than try to ease the weighty picture up over the tightly fixed rod work. The builders began the work that was to last a week.

By Friday of that week they had finished and they advised that no one should enter the room until the chemicals and plaster dust had settled down.

On the following Monday morning Roy came in early to open up for the builders so they could begin some re-plastering work but what greeted him was something of a shock.

'To my horror the portrait of the Green Lady was on the floor. It had come off the wall. I had checked it was all okay when I locked up for the weekend. Now the portrait was on the floor and there was some damage to it and the frame was broken in various places as well. When I came in I thought there had been a burglary or something like that.'

He checked all the windows and they were firmly shut and he was the only key holder. He knew no one had been able to enter that room over the weekend. Then he noticed that the thick layer of plaster dust that had settled over the weekend was totally undisturbed.

'There were no footprints,' Roy told me, 'nor anything in the dust – it was just as it was when we left it. It fact it had got thicker, as more dust had settled over the weekend. To this day I don't know what caused the Green Lady's portrait to come down at all, it couldn't just fall – there is no way – I had not touched it.'

The picture rods were still protruding from the wall – so the portrait, as with Sir Peter's, would need to be lifted up fairly high before being freed from the brackets and Roy knew how tightly welded they had been over the years.

'Now, to this day I have no explanation as to how that could have happened – it cost us about £400 to repair and restore it. So that is one thing I have no explanation of.'

The portrait's position, face down on the floor, was directly above the cellar where Sir Peter's portrait was stored, awaiting its return alongside her. It seems the Green Lady did not take kindly to being left alone once more without her beloved Peter – and in death, as well as life, she made her feelings known.

Before we leave Woodrow High House, there is one more tale to tell and it hints very strongly that there is another restless spirit in the house. Again it was experienced by Roy but in a totally unexpected way. One day he received a telephone call from a senior citizens' luncheon club in London asking if they could come down and visit the house. Roy remembers the call well because the woman who phoned said to him, 'We've phoned your County Council and asked if you've got any stately homes or historic buildings in your area and they gave us one or two but they are really expensive.' Then she continued, 'They said Woodrow High House might let us come out for a day trip and we could have a little tour and a talk and it wouldn't cost us much.'

Roy agreed to organise it for them at a time when there were no children about and on the appointed day about 20 elderly ladies and two equally-elderly gentlemen arrived in a small coach from London.

Roy takes up the story. 'As they came in the entrance hall, one of the old ladies stood dead still in her tracks – she suddenly stopped and went into this trance-like state saying, "Oh my gaud, oh my gaud, there are three spirits in this house – three spirits I tell yer."

'I fetched her a glass of water because she was frozen in this trance-like state. Then she carried on, "Oh my gaud, I see three spirits, I see a lady of noble birth, and a gentleman of a military persuasion and I see a child, and the child is crying."

'Meanwhile, everyone else had shuffled past into the Assembly Room and they sat round in a circle – they had cups of tea and we did movements to music – a kind of welcome bit of fun.

'Eventually the lady came in, and she immediately identified the two people she had seen whilst in a trance as Lady Helena Stanhope and Sir Peter Bostock by their portraits on the wall. We just laughed at it really. Then somebody said, "Where's the child then? You don't have a portrait of a child." '

The old lady explained to all that she had seen a child dressed in calico and it was crying. Roy knew that as calico is unbleached cotton it would have been worn primarily by poor children and certainly would not be connected to Lady Helena Stanhope and Sir Peter Bostock. Also poor children wouldn't have had their portraits painted so there would be no easy identification of the distressed child she claimed to have seen.

'Anyway,' recalled Roy, 'we all had a wry grin on our faces and all went out in the garden. It was a nice day, and they eventually went home, back to London and I never heard anything from them again.'

It was just after they'd gone that Roy suddenly stopped in his tracks and goose bumps crept up the back of his neck. He had totally forgotten. The crying child seen by the old lady! For some reason he had not made the connection with an event that had occurred some 18 months previously.

'It was in the winter, January, something like that – and I was working late in the evening, and my office used to be a little room on the landing. I'm here late at night typing letters out on an old typewriter. Suddenly I heard what seemed to be a child calling out. There was nobody in residence, being January.

'I heard this child's voice crying, rather like a child trying to call through sobbing, trying to catch their breath. I immediately thought, "God, there's been an accident at home and it's my youngest daughter calling me." I had two children at that time, one was ten and the other would have been six coming up seven. I thought the eldest one had run up to the main house where I was working, we lived in a house in the grounds, because something has happened at home. So in a bit of a panic, I ran out, switching on the landing lights shouting, "Jane where are you, what's the matter?" I ran down the stairs, it just went silent. I searched around a bit downstairs – picked up the phone, rang my wife, and said, "What's happened, where are the children?"

'She said, "Well they are in bed sound asleep." So I said, "Are you absolutely sure?" So she said, "Yes of course I am." I said, "I'm sure I heard Jane up here."

'She asked me to explain, but I said I hadn't got time as I wanted to go and have a look round. So I put the phone down, got a torch and went downstairs and also looked outside the building, but found nothing. The sobbing had been very clear and quite loud. So I went home, explained what had happened to my wife then forgot all about it until that day when we had that luncheon club visit.

'Even now it gives me goose bumps on the back of my neck. As soon as that lady arrived she had started talking about a child and the child was sobbing, and now the two things suddenly linked.'

Is there a child at Woodrow High House whose story is yet to be uncovered and connects to Lady Helena Stanhope and Sir Peter Bostock? I certainly intend to find out, but that will have to wait for the next book.

11

Glory Mill Fred – The Grumpy DIY Ghost

YOUNG married couple Julie and Jimmy Harmen had at long last found a house they could afford. It was a tad dilapidated and needed a lot of work but it was a bargain. Situated in Glory Mill Lane close to Wooburn Green and the Rye, it was a picturesque, rural location back in 1972.

Julie put its scruffy interior down to the fact that it had changed hands around eight times in only a dozen or so years. Nobody seemed to want to make it a home to settle down in. Julie and Jimmy were determined to transform this Victorian semi into a real home, and with their daughter Claire coming up to five years old, it had plenty of space for a growing family.

Before they moved into the empty house Julie set time aside to try and clean it up before they went to live there permanently.

'It was an awful mess,' Julie told me, 'and so very cold.'

As Julie visited the house to try and make it more habitable, she found the temperature far too cold to tolerate for very long. But it was more than just the cold that bothered her. The whole atmosphere was oppressive. It was as if she was unwelcome and the house itself just wanted her out. She tried to ignore this 'unfriendly sensation', as she called it, but after half an hour or so it became so powerful, she had to leave.

Jimmy told her not to be silly. It was just a cold house in need of the attention which they would soon give. Julie persevered with her pre-move work but each time she would stay as short a time as possible.

Moving-in day arrived and they worked hard arranging their possessions and furnishing their bedroom for their first cosy night in their new home. Thanks to Julie's hard work, it was as clean as it was ever going to be but the tatty, depressing wallpaper and dowdy lino was earmarked for change as soon as their income allowed it. That first night they snuggled up in bed for warmth. Claire was tucked up in her new bedroom, which was a side-room off mum and dad's.

It was a new start – albeit in a house that needed a daunting amount of work. But they were young and enthusiastic and they were determined to transform their Glory Mill Lane purchase into a real family home.

Exhausted after a long day, they lay together and drifted off to sleep. Then they woke again with a start. There was a noise downstairs. They could hear the front door open, the sound of someone walking into the hall and closing the door after them. They sat up, frightened and startled. Someone must have a set of keys, what on earth was going on?

Fright turned to horror as slowly, but surely, someone began to climb the stairs – deliberate, tired, echoing footsteps coming closer and closer …

Too scared to even move, they listened as the footsteps reached the landing and went along to the front bedroom. They heard the bedroom door open and then shut firmly behind whoever (or whatever) was now inside their front bedroom.

With a feeling of apprehension, tinged with indignation that someone still had a key to their house and was lodging there, Jimmy crept along to confront the intruder. All he had to hand was a rolled-up newspaper. He flung open the door and shouted, 'What do you think you are doing?'

There was silence. The room was empty. Cautiously peering around the door, Jimmy saw that there was no one in the room, absolutely no one at all. The window was firmly shut and downstairs the front door was locked.

A restless night ensued – eventually drifting into early morning sleepy confusion – was last night's intrusion a dream? Then, in the haze of their early morning slumber, they heard the same deliberate tread, the same footsteps begin again as someone made their way down the stairs and out of the front door.

Jimmy ran to catch them, the morning light giving him courage for any confrontation. There was no one on the stairs. The front door remained locked from the inside.

Jimmy and Julie now struggled to understand what had gone on. It made no sense. Each had heard the same sounds and each had seen that no one was there. They re-checked the empty front bedroom – it remained empty with no sign of anyone using it overnight. They were worried and confused, but relieved that Claire was safe in the room adjoining theirs.

Thus began what became a regular event for Jimmy and Julie. Fred, as they called him, came in every night and left every morning.

If they stayed up to watch, nothing happened. When they were in their bedroom or even in the kitchen, the sound of the front door opening and footsteps climbing the stairs to the front bedroom happened every day. Yet there was no one there, no doors were left open, there was no sign of any visitor – yet!

It was unnaturally cold in the stairwell and when you reached the very top of the stairs there was always a distinctive smell. Julie described it as a mixture of cloves and sweet-scented carnations.

It now became clear why this house had had so many owners in such a short space of time. But remarkably, Jimmy and Julie decided to stay and tackle their ghost head on, too much effort had gone into buying this house. They now knew why it was cheaper than similar houses nearby – people had wanted to get shot of it quickly.

Claire was clearly a happy little girl and not worried by Fred's presence but did have one complaint. Not long after moving in, she said to her mum, 'Mummy can you stop those children making such a noise, they are waking me up.'

Claire, now in her forties, told me that she could clearly hear the sounds of children playing and chatting at the end of her bed but mum and dad never heard it at all. Julie also recalls their neighbour Nigel calling round to complain about Claire and 'the other children' keeping his daughter Karen awake at night with their chatter and laughter, which could be heard through the dividing wall. He was startled to learn that, in fact, Claire was on holiday in Cornwell with Julie's parents at the time and no one else was sleeping in that room on the night in question. Claire also recalls Fred's footsteps thumping up the stairs and dad leaping out of bed, putting on the light, but all would be silence when he went to investigate. He would get back into bed and the footsteps would start again. 'It was a unique house,' she added as an afterthought. Judging from what now follows, it certainly was.

It soon became apparent to Jimmy and Julie that Fred was very particular about his house being left as it was. Attempts to strip and replace the old layers of wallpaper or make alterations of any kind began to be met with supernatural anger. This would manifest itself as ornaments being flung across the room, usually in the direction of Jimmy rather than Julie. Fred would also make loud crashing noises as they started to strip away the layers of wallpaper. Julie recalls one incident in the newly decorated lounge.

Jimmy had put two ornamental guns on display above the fireplace. While they were having coffee with some friends, the guns left the wall and were hurled across the room, terrifying everybody. It was a miracle no one was injured.

When they had completed an archway into the sitting room and decorated it with pictures – they were flung off directly at Jimmy. One day, he was hit by a flying vase that smashed on contact with the side of his head.

In a bizarre attempt to confront what seemed to have the hallmarks of a poltergeist haunting, Jimmy and Julie decided to discuss their plans for doing up the house with their supernatural lodger. This meant they now had to fully accept that if they continued to live at their Glory Mill home, they were not alone. So from that decisive moment, they thought it best to acknowledge his presence and include Fred in their discussions. They asked him to stop the children making a noise by Claire's bed and indeed it stopped.

They openly discussed taking down a dividing wall to create an open-plan lounge and – as crazy as it sounds – they asked Fred's permission. Nothing happened, no vases flew through the air, which they took as approval.

One Sunday, Owen, a builder friend of Jimmy's, screened off the area with a large sheet and began taking down the internal wall. The work went well and Jimmy and Julie were grateful there were no incidents, no temper tantrums from Fred.

Owen shouted out that he was off to the pub for his lunch and would be back to finish clearing up that afternoon. After Owen said he was off, Jimmy and Julie and Claire, then 8 years old and used to Fred's presence, could still hear him at work, sweeping and shovelling up the rubble. Jimmy called out, 'You still here Owen?' But there was no answer. They peered around the sheet and there was nothing there but a neatly swept concrete floor and pile of rubble waiting to be taken away. Fred had decided Owen needed a hand.

Claire told me about growing up with Fred. 'My clearest recollection,' she said, 'was when we had two rooms knocked into one. We had an archway put in. It was Sunday lunchtime and we were sitting down eating dinner at the table and I remember dad saying that Owen was working late. We could hear the sweeping in the front room. Owen had definitely left all his dust and rubble scattered in the room and when he came back it was all cleared away.'

I asked Claire if she was scared and she said she did not know any different.

'It was a strange house,' she told me, 'the front bedroom was always very cold. I think the only person who ever slept there was my grandfather when he came to stay. As he only came up in the summer he probably thought it was just nice and cool.'

Jimmy, Julie and Claire had become used to Fred and his comings and goings and occasional angry outbursts. They spent eight years at Glory Mill Lane, transforming it into a comfortable family home complete with a supernatural lodger. Claire clearly remembers her dad's bedtime ritual. Every night he would say, 'Come on Fred, we're going to bed now!'

In trying to find out who Fred might be, Jimmy and Julie had been told that there had been a fire in the house many years ago and a woman had died there. Was Fred perhaps Freda? They had wondered what happened in the past when they stripped back the layers of wallpaper and discovered the plaster walls were black with a sooty deposit indicating such a fire had indeed taken place.

The story does not end at this point – far from it. They sold the house to their friends Dougie and Sandra, but neglected to mention Fred. It was their secret.

'We are leaving!' they shouted to Fred and that same day their friends moved in. Claire recalls Fred having the last word when in response to their farewells, the kitchen clock shot off the wall flying some distance across the room.

It wasn't long before Dougie confronted them, saying, 'You didn't tell us there is somebody else living here!'

'We didn't want to worry you,' said Julie.

This could have been the end of a friendship but it wasn't and they were able to share experiences of living with Fred. Unfortunately, Dougie and Sandra soon parted ways – nothing to do with Fred, however. Dougie was now living there alone. Working as a baker he would not go to bed late in the evening as he had such an early start.

One night, he was violently shaken awake by an unseen hand.

The room and landing were full of black smoke. He rushed downstairs where his dogs were sleeping and found that the paraffin stove had a fault and instead of cutting right out had been billowing sooty black smoke. The dogs were safe, if a little grubby, but the carpet all around the heater was burnt away.

Had Fred (or Freda?) saved their lives that night? If so, he (or she) soon took exception to Dougie's hobby of Citizens' Band Radio which involved many hours talking to other enthusiasts. It became a craze after the mid-1970s song *Convoy* – a conversation between three truckers, using their handles 'Rubber Duck', 'Pig Pen' and 'Sod Buster'.

Dougie had mounted all his weighty transmission equipment on special rawbolts in the wall on heavy-duty shelving capable of taking a tremendous loading.

One day Dougie came home to find it had been ripped clean away from the wall. It had not fallen, that would be well nigh impossible, but it had been pulled away some distance by force. This could have become serious, so like Jimmy and Julie, he also took Fred into his confidence and managed eight years at that same haunted address, always careful to explain to Fred what he was planning to do.

Once these episodes became more talked about, it was clear that others knew about the haunting. Julie learnt that a previous owner, Mrs Stotter, had called him Sticker. 'Get out of my way, Sticker,' she would say. She had thought that his footsteps up and down the stairs sounded as if he had a toffee paper stuck to his boot.

Sticker, Fred or Freda? As Claire so aptly remarked, 'It was a unique house.'

12

Buckingham: The Supernatural Legacy of St Rumbold

THE DEATH of a three-day-old Mercian prince in approximately AD 650 left a remarkable ecclesiastical legacy in the town of Buckingham. His name was Rumbold and it is said his father was Alchfrith, son of the king of Northumbria, and his mother was Cyneburga, daughter of Penda who was the king of Mercia. Little scepticism therefore was given to the claim that a child of such royal parentage was so special that on the day he was born he is said to have proclaimed in a loud voice, not once, but three times, 'I am a Christian.' And he sought to be baptised as such. His power at one-day-old was so remarkable that he commanded a stone bowl be brought to him in which he was duly baptised. The bowl was too heavy to be lifted until he demanded it, only then was it possible to bring it to him for the baptism.

He spent his second day of life preaching a Christian sermon and predicted his own death on the third day of life. He decreed that after interment for one year at King's Sutton where he was born, then for two years at Brackley, his final resting place should be Buckingham.

Rumbold was canonised and his tomb and shrine near the old church in Buckingham became a place of pilgrimage.

This legacy led to the establishment of many ecclesiastical dedications to the infant Rumbold and, in particular, a well, the waters from which were claimed to cure the lame, the blind and all manner of sickness and malformations of the body.

Now, given the fantastic claims concerning the powers of St Rumbold's Well in Buckingham, many of the public houses in the vicinity became inundated with travellers and pilgrims and took on the important role of 'ecclesiastical inns'. They looked after the pilgrims with food and shelter and plenty of alcohol to fuel their religious fervour and they were often packed to the gunnels with celebrating patrons. The pub names would reflect their religious connections. Names such as the Mitre, and the Cross Keys (the emblem of St Peter) were extremely popular in the Lenborough and Prebend End areas where the principal well was situated. The Cross Keys inn claimed the closest proximity and would use the basement area to house passing travellers with 'bed and board' – the board being a wooden platter on which the food was served.

Today, the Cross Keys has been converted into two semi-detached houses and is hardly recognisable as the inn that saw so many travellers pass through its doors. The question is, are there still one or two travellers lingering on all these years later, waiting to pay their respects to St Rumbold?

I spoke with Norma and Bernard who used to live there in the early 1970s. Norma told me, 'Our children were quite young when we moved in 1972. Our eldest daughter was away at university and our twins Adrian and Kathryn were still at home. They used to be woken up by someone walking about, up and down the stairs. We used to sleep through it, so we thought they were joking and we didn't take it seriously.'

However, Adrian and Kathryn were deadly serious. The constant sound of these heavy footsteps at night was also accompanied by the clanking noise a sword might make, its scabbard mount hitting the metal stud of the wearer's belt. They were really fearful of this prowling sound, yet nothing was seen and Norma and Bernard were never disturbed by it.

Norma told me that a young mother and her three-year-old son who moved into the other semi did not stay very long. She thinks she now knows why, and appreciates a little more what her own twins had been experiencing.

She said that next door there were four steps that went down into a back room with a stone floor. It was probably used for storing ale or to house travellers in busy periods. It had now been converted into a playroom for the little lad but he did not want to go in there and would get quite upset.

Norma told me that his mother used to say, 'For goodness sake, get away from under my feet, you are always hanging round me, go and play in your playroom.' But the little boy said to her, on numerous occasions, 'No mummy, I don't like going down there because I don't like the man that's sitting in the chair staring at me.'

And she said, 'What man?' because she couldn't see a man.

He said, 'He's a funny man because he wears funny clothes.'

'What do you mean he wears funny clothes?'

'Well, he's got a lump of metal down the side of him!'

Norma presumed he meant the sword. 'I think he did also say he had a feather in his hat. We were quite relieved when he seemed to leave us and wasn't with us any more.'

However, one evening Norma and Bernard had been entertaining their good friend Pauline. She was about to set off home and Bernard fetched her heavy sheepskin coat. As he handed it to her – intending to help her on with it – he was momentarily distracted, he can't explain why.

'Thank you Bernard,' Pauline said.

'What for?' Bernard asked.

'For helping me on with my coat.'

'Sorry Pauline, I was distracted, I would have done it but I didn't touch it,' replied Bernard.

But Pauline wasn't being sarcastic, she really meant 'thank you', precisely because someone had helped her on with her coat. Norma recalls how Pauline sat back down again and went quite white.

'Somebody helped me put my coat on and if it wasn't you, who was it?'

He may be noisy at night and scare little boys from their playroom but he appears to have impeccable manners – whoever he is.

13

The Gentle Young Ghosts
of Pinewood and Denham

B ERYL BUTLER loved her job at Pinewood Film Studios at Iver
Heath in Buckinghamshire. The studios were buzzing with
anticipation as they re-opened after wartime closure on Monday 8
April 1946. Beryl was beginning what would become a 38-year
career, starting at the studio's busy switchboard as a telephonist.

Pinewood Studios had become a world-renowned studio –
celebrating its tenth birthday since the building tycoon Charles
Boot, in partnership with J. Arthur Rank, turned a luxurious
mansion house called Heatherden Hall into a unique countryside
film complex in 1936.

Now the war was over, Pinewood's reputation for producing
Oscar-winning films was being firmly established with some early
post-war classics. Frank Lauder and Sidney Gilliat's *Green for Danger*
was the first film in production after Pinewood started up again.
This was followed by *Great Expectations* and *Black Narcissus* – both
Oscar winners. Truly an exhilarating time to be a young woman
enjoying the excitement and glamour of the film world and being
close to actors such as John Mills, Valerie Hobson, Alistair Sim, Sally
Gray and Sabu who were to become legendary.

At this time Beryl was swept along with the sheer speed of
Pinewood's growth, her own area of work in telecommunications
was fast evolving with the advent of the teleprinter and later the fax
machine. From telephonist to supervisor to telecommunications
manager – her career flourished and by the late 1970s she, now in
her fifties, loved her job as much as ever.

One very important part of her working life was her appreciation of the beautiful and much filmed Heatherden House – retained as the core historic feature of the studio setting. The main house evolved as a crucial period setting for a whole raft of evocative Victorian or Edwardian themed films as well as housing the management and communication services of Pinewood Studios. The outside car parks and hangar-style lots stood in stark contrast to this magnificent mansion at the centre of the studio complex.

One busy day in 1979, Beryl was alone, working late in the teleprinter room. There were deadlines to meet and it was easier to stay on and work after the hectic rush of the day. As she dealt with the urgent documents, she sensed that someone was close by. Turning around she was startled to see a most beautiful young girl standing in the open doorway.

Beryl was transfixed by her tumbling blonde hair, her exquisite Edwardian blouse of broderie anglaise with a flannel skirt, so very narrow at the waist, flaring out to show the most elaborate white satin petticoat. This was a moment frozen in time as they looked at each other.

There was no period-costume filming that day, certainly no children on sets anywhere, and no one should have been in the building anyway. Beryl, now in her 80s and recalling this moment, told me that the girl was about 7 or 8 years old and was 'the most beautiful child I have ever seen'. There was a tear in her eye, and a tremble in her voice as she recalled the peaceful, still moment of this unexpected encounter.

No words were spoken. Then slowly, the child faded away leaving Beryl staring in disbelief at the open doorway. It was a moment that would never be forgotten.

There was also a strange familiarity about this beautiful, angelic child and it nagged her subconscious. A few days later, as she walked down what was called the South Corridor, adorned with art from the original owners of Heatherden Hall, she once more felt that tingle of being watched. She went into the Green Room and there above the fireplace was a portrait of that same child, sitting on the lawns of the house with two bounding dogs playing at her side.

It was as startling as it was familiar – was this the explanation? She had subconsciously conjured up the image from having previously seen the painting over many years working close by. Yet the clothes, Beryl recalled, were not those she was wearing in the portrait and there had been much more poignancy in her expression, a sadness not apparent in the painting where she was happy and playing.

Eventually, Beryl confided to an elderly friend about her experience. Far from dismissing Beryl's experience as a hallucination or her vivid imagination, she went very quiet and then, asking Beryl to wait a minute, she left the room.

Beryl heard her searching, opening and shutting drawers, and soon she returned clutching a yellowing newspaper cutting. Her friend used to work as a servant in the house and the brief paragraph described how a young girl of the family at Heatherden Hall was excited about going on a trip and hearing the approaching coach and horses, she rushed outside and tripped over, panicking the horses.

She was crushed by the carriage wheels as the horses bolted.

They both went quiet for a moment. Beryl's description of the little girl exactly matched the old lady's memory of her and was indeed the same as the girl in the portrait.

But why had she appeared in the doorway of the teleprinter room? When Beryl returned to work she discovered that the way in which the house had been altered when Charles Boot re-vamped the whole layout to accommodate his project for the film studios, the teleprinter doorway was the original front door of the house where the road ran past to the stables. The very road the carriage would have taken to collect an excited young girl for her outing.

Beryl retired from Pinewood in 1984 but has never, ever forgotten 'the most delightful child you ever saw'.

Local celebrity Cilla Black also met a gentle young ghost at her Buckinghamshire home in nearby Denham. I spoke with the well-known journalist Richard Barber, who had very recently interviewed

Cilla about this experience and he kindly gave me permission to reproduce her story, as published in the *Daily Mail Weekend* magazine on 19th January, 2008.

'About ten years ago,' Cilla told Richard, 'I woke up in the middle of the night and a girl was standing next to my bed. I wasn't in the least bit scared. There was a good feeling about her, a positive aura. And she was absolutely clear to me. She had long hair and was wearing a sort of Laura Ashley-style nightdress. I later discovered she was the 14-year-old daughter of one of the estate workers and she died in 1912. Her funeral cortège to the village church started from my house.'

She then told Richard that the young girl had appeared again by her side on at least two more occasions but her husband Bobby could not see her. 'I woke Bobby up on one occasion,' she told Richard, 'but he couldn't see her and, funnily enough, she's never appeared since he died in 1999.' Since this experience Cilla has become more and more interested in psychic phenomena and, like Beryl at Pinewood, will never forget her encounter with such a gentle ghost.

14

Highway Encounters of the Supernatural Kind

SOME supernatural events occur in such unexpected ways that it is only afterwards that the impact of what happened can haunt you. If you go into a dark, creepy house, or play with a Ouija board, or frequent anywhere known to be ghostly, then real or imaginary apparitions, sounds and eerie happenings are already in context. But this is where we are fooling ourselves. There is no special context for a supernatural event. Culturally, we tend towards the Hallowe'en version of the supernatural – spooky places, the toll of the midnight bell, spectres of evil and wailing ghosts.

Many of the stories and experiences I have encountered are the exact opposite of this. It is in the mundane, the routine context of everyday life that a supernatural occurrence can pass by – literally.

A passing shadow, a shade, a glimpse of something that just vanishes or melts away. You are left never quite sure of exactly what you have experienced but you know it was something out of the ordinary.

When you are with another person and you both experience such an event then it does become a serious matter for consideration.

Writer, presenter, and collector of ghost stories, Vivienne Rae-Ellis recorded a masterly example of what she, in her book *True Ghost Stories of Our Own Time*, classifies as a highway encounter that involved not one but up to four people experiencing the same apparition – the same scary experience of being involved in an accident when all was not quite as it seemed.

She recounts the experience of Bill Smith and his lorry-driver mate, passing through Buckinghamshire en route to Worcester in December 1936. It is a two-driver run, so they could take turns at the wheel. The night was foggy between Uxbridge and High Wycombe along the A40. Bill was steadily negotiating the gradient of White Hill – peering through the fog as his headlights bounced back at him from the grey blanket outside.

Bill's mate, alert to the dangerous driving conditions, suddenly spotted a figure dressed in a long black cloak stepping in front of their lorry. Reproduced with Vivienne's kind permission, this is exactly what the driver Bill Smith was able to tell her.

'Suddenly my driver mate shouted, "Look out! You'll hit him!" and into the beam of the headlights stepped a figure in a long black cloak. I braked hard, but was unable to stop before he disappeared beneath my radiator cowling. My mate opened his door and jumped out as the lorry came to a halt. I switched off the engine, engaged reverse and set the handbrake for safety. As I got out, my mate was coming along the roadside looking underneath the truck saying, "Where the hell is he! He must be hung up underneath, poor bugger. He must have been blind to walk into us like that."

'I couldn't answer. I had the smell of death in my nostrils, and I was freezing cold. I leaned against the lorry not daring to even think. I knew in my mind we should find nothing. My mate put his hand on my shoulder and said, "It wasn't your fault Bill. No one could have avoided him. He just walked straight into us!"

'I reached into the lorry for my torch. He took it from me and crawled underneath the vehicle, shone it around, and shouted, "There's nothing under here." He came out and started back up the road where there were several skid marks. He went beyond them, then came back on the offside of the road, saying, "There's nothing there! Where can he have gone?"

'We looked at the roadside which was banked as a cutting so he could not have been thrown off the road altogether. I knew, but I could not tell my mate, that we had seen something which wasn't there ...' (Rae-Ellis, V. *True Ghost Stories of Our Own Time* Faber & Faber, London 1990.)

Bill then went on to explain to Vivienne how they were anxious to report the accident to the police so they continued on their way and, on spotting a policeman in High Wycombe, pulled over and described what had happened. The policeman, rather than reacting positively, appeared exasperated and said to Bill, 'What game are you blokes playing tonight? You're the third driver who has knocked somebody over who can't be found! We had a patrol car up there searching for an hour but they found nothing, and now you have the same tale! You're asking for trouble, wasting police time to chase shadows.'

Bill and his friend, still in a state of shock, after their experience and at the reaction of the policeman, set off towards Oxford.

Bill continues, 'As we ran out of West Wycombe towards Oxford we saw a lorry stopped and a driver with a wheel off. We pulled in behind to give him the benefit of our lights and got out. As we approached he straightened up and said, "Can you hear singing, or am I going daft?" We listened. We could hear a church service somewhere, but no organ music.'

Vivienne writes, 'The music appeared to be coming from the earth bank across the road and all the men could hear the sound which appeared to be a congregation or choir singing hymns although the words were "strange and unintelligible". The other driver was relieved when Mr Smith and his mate agreed that they, too, could hear the music, but could find no explanation for it. The other man begged them not to pull his leg.

'"I'm bloody scared," he admitted, "I knocked a bloke down other side of Wycombe. When I looked for him he wasn't there. I told the coppers and went up there with them for an hour but we couldn't find anything, only skid marks on the road; and then the coppers said I was drunk and they would pull me in for time-wasting. I don't drink and I don't smoke. But I know I saw a bloke walk into my front. He came from nowhere and he disappeared the same. I had a good look, he was dressed like a monk in a long cloak with a hood over his head.'"

Bill and his mate were able to reassure the driver that exactly the same experience had befallen them. The lorry driver then said that when he pulled over to change the wheel, 'I was listening when a lorry pulled up behind me. The driver was scared stiff, he reckoned he had knocked a bloke down and when I told him about the singing, he wouldn't stop no longer.'

Vivienne writes, 'Bill Smith and his mate, shaken by the latest revelation, helped the driver change his wheel and followed him to Witney where they parted company.'

Bill recalled, 'We never stopped talking and wondering about what we had seen and heard for the rest of the journey. We were laughed at and ridiculed when we told people about it. But we knew we had witnessed an apparition and heard singing, although we had no way of finding out what it was.'

*****

Arju Miah, a Milton Keynes cab driver based in Cosgrove, is still haunted by a ghostly experience that defies explanation.

He was booked to pick up a fare outside the Sanctuary nightclub in Denbigh in the early hours of New Year's Day 2001. It was around 3.45 am when a striking young woman got into the back of his cab.

Arju described her as having pink hair, wearing a short black skirt and a white shirt. She proved to be very chatty and she told him how she had been out with friends who had booked a limousine but she wanted to leave earlier as she was tired.

As he left Buckinghamshire and was approaching Bedford, he couldn't see the young woman in his mirror and thought she'd fallen asleep, slumping down into the footwell. He pulled over to discover there was no one sitting in the back of his cab at all. He was astounded. More so because he had already been paid with new £20 notes.

Arju told the *Milton Keynes Citizen* newspaper, 'Now I think back, her hand was very cold when she gave me the money. She told me it was because she had been waiting in the cold, but she had not been waiting that long. Other people in cabs saw her get in as well. There's just no explanation. I don't know who she was. She was nothing but a ghost. I can think of no other explanation.'

Ghostly passengers, jaywalkers, passers-by and other casual encounters are recorded time and time again in the annals of supernatural events.

Why such a spiritual energy should be preoccupied in this way is a subject for argument. What Frederick Myers, founder of the Society for Psychical Research, defined as 'a manifestation of persistent personal energy' is often place-centred and will re-appear time and time again and, as in the case of Bill Smith and his fellow drivers, be knocked down time and time again – except not being of earthly flesh they are not even in the same dimension as the travelling vehicle so they were never struck in the first place. The most famous supernatural case of this type is associated with Kent and is known as the ghost of Blue Bell Hill. Over the years, well over 24 independent witnesses have reported colliding with a young woman who had stared calmly into their horrified eyes as they crashed into her. She is supposedly a woman killed on the eve of her wedding in 1965 and is a regular 'victim' of a non-existent accident.

However, explaining a chatty, cab-riding, fashionable young woman, who leaves real twenty pound notes then melts away as a ghost, is difficult, but it is part of a long supernatural legacy associated with phantom hitchhikers. Andrew Lang, also associated with the Society of Psychical Research says, 'People will unconsciously localise old legends in new places and assign old occurrences to new persons.'

So, did Arju Miah just re-invent a new 'urban legend'? He is absolutely clear that it was a real and unnerving experience.

The Buckinghamshire hamlet of Wheeler End Common and the nearby village of Lane End have a long-standing supernatural story of the Lady in Red who will cross the path of a strolling pedestrian from time to time. Nothing startling such as an accident, but a distinct apparition that fades away to reveal she is not of this world. She is said to be Anna who fell ill and died two weeks before her wedding day in 1776.

Well into the 20th century, however, her distinct red, flowing 18th-century costume has also surprised countryside walkers on Hanover Hill close to Bolter End – the last reported sighting was in the cold winter weather of December 1973.

Certain casual encounters with the supernatural are so understated that they appear almost normal but still leave that nagging need for explanation in the observer's mind.

John Bushell is one such observer and he told me about a particular night when he was working as a security guard at what used to be the Bowyers sausage and pie factory in Amersham on the A413 London Road – the site is now a Tesco car park.

It was early New Year's Day in 1974 and he was standing on the junction by Station Road, looking towards London Road West in the direction of the Chequers pub fronted by the old Amersham watermill.

He was with his guard dog Max who suddenly stiffened, growled and looked up towards Station Road. John was conscious of a man walking slowly across the road to his left, having come alongside the river Misbourne, from the direction of Martyrs' Field, where in the 16th century seven local Lollard men and one woman were burnt at the stake – the so-called Amersham Martyrs (see Chapter 5).

John and his dog watched silently as the man headed towards the other side of the road where there was a large yew tree on the green. What was so remarkable for John was the clear image of a man from another era. His dark, high-collared coat and fitted worsted trousers were not of the 20th century and his long grey-flecked hair was tied back at the nape of the neck in the style of the late 17th or early 18th century.

His head was bent forward as if he were deep in thought as he headed directly towards the yew tree. John and the dog watched as he disappeared, hidden by the low bushy branches of the tree. John waited to see him re-emerge on the other side of the large grassy area around the tree, interested to see where he would be heading next. However, he never did re-emerge from behind the branches – he should have been back in sight within seconds, not minutes. For some reason he had decided to stay hidden by the tree. John crossed over the road to investigate – he looked and looked but there was absolutely no one in sight. The man had completely vanished although he could not have moved away from the tree without being seen. The guard dog was excitedly sniffing around the tree area but they could find no human form hiding within its shelter.

Ever since that experience, John has tried to find an everyday explanation – but how? It was an unexpected encounter and because of his observations and the definite reaction of the dog, it seemed to be a real encounter, not one of the imagination. The clothing and posture were so striking yet they did not seem to have a connection with the 16th-century Amersham Martyrs. The man seemed to be from at least a century or more later than that period. John's own research into the man's appearance dates him from around the very early years of the 19th century but it is only guess-work. What was certainly not guesswork was where he finished his journey that night – at and not beyond the yew tree.

The yew is a powerful supernatural symbol of death and rebirth. Many cultures, particularly that of England in the period when archery was an important battle skill, revered the yew tree for its special strengths and versatility in making bows. It also has another accolade – for some it is the 'door of heaven'.

For John it is a supernatural encounter without an end – a snippet of time that has no natural niche to rest comfortably in his mind – just a personal, inconclusive, but nonetheless real experience.

'Seeing is believing' has to be the motto here.

So who did John see on that early morning in Amersham? Somehow I think that question will remain in the air.

15

Drayton Parslow and the Salden Pond Ghost

HEADLESS GHOSTS are, of course, an essential ingredient in folklore and supernatural tales. Indeed, J.K. Rowling's *Harry Potter* series gave an additional twist to the headless ghost genre with the creation of Gryffindor's resident ghost – Nearly Headless Nick. The 45 blunt axe blows of his botched execution left his head attached by a mere flap of skin and sinew, leading him to lament, 'My faithful old head, it never saw fit to desert me.'

Humour, it seems, remains a close companion of what is clearly a terrible fate and, in Buckinghamshire, Horace Harman discovered the story of the Salden ghost which again takes on a certain light touch, especially when recounted in the local dialect which was Harman's speciality. The following story uses extracts from a longer conversation recorded by Harman in 1929 on a stormy night in a pub at Drayton Parslow. I have christened them Jim and Chawley as Harman used only 'A' and 'B' to distinguish these two wonderful Buckinghamshire characters.

*****

Chawley What a night! 'Tis as dark as pitch. I a jest come up the road and I dint know how to find mi way. I got in the hedge once or twice as I was a-tryin to git out a the way a the pond. This is, I think, about one a the darkest nights as ivver I was in. I could jist see the trees in the hedgerows agenst the sky, and what with the wind a-blowin in the branches and the noise they made, I felt quite creepy as I come up. I shoont like to git fur afeeuld to-night.

Jim You ought to goo down to Sauldin [Salden] an a night like this. That's wheeur you ought to goo, and then ood see summut.

Chawley What?

Jim Sauldin's a rum ole pleeace, Sauldin is. 'Tis a rum ole pleeace, I tell ye!

Chawley What do you see?

Jim Why, a ole fellur with his feeace under his arm – he comes out an a night like this. I tell ye, 'tis a rum ole pleeace!

Chawley A you sin him?

Jim Ant I begad – many a time!

Chawley What does he do?

Jim Well I ull tell ye. When you git down tuther side a Sauldin pond an a night like this, and you be a-gooin an the road, thaiur's an ole fellur as comes and walks by yur side – thaiur he is a-gooin an by the side an ye, and thaiur's he old feeace under his arm a-looking at ye all the time, and he keeps an till he gits to a certain pleeace and then he leeavs ye. He walks by yur side all the time and nivver speeaks.

Chawley Don't ye crack him an the head wi yur stick?

Jim No, begad; I allus let him alooan; these things be best let alooan. Besides, he never hurts ye. Many a time has he bin by mi side and he nivver does nauthing. If ye were to follur him, I rickun he ood taiak ye to a pleeace wheeur thaiur's a pot of money or summut like that; but thaiur aint anybody has got the pluck to goo wi him.

Chawley When did you see him fust?

Jim One dark night when I was wi ole Tom Kirk. We were an tuther side a the pond when ole Tom says to me, 'Look out Jim, heear he is!' And thaiur he was too, a-walkin by the side an us. My heear stood on end and lifted mi cap right up. I tell ye I had got the wind up properly. There he kep an by the side an us with his old feeace under his arm a-looking at us.

Chawley What did ole Tom do?

Jim   Nauthin. All he said was, 'Let him alooan. Taiak no no-atice an him!' Ole Tom had sin him many a time, so he was quite used to him. He lived just tuther side a the pond and had walked the rooad all the times a night, so he dint mind him. I ull taiak ye down to Sauldin pond one a these dark nights. Will you goo?

Chawley   Yis, I ull. What's the time?

Jim   Why gittin an.

Chawley   I shull have to make a move.

Jim   So shull I.

Chawley   I hope I don't meet the ole fellur down the rooad.

Jim   He dooant git as fur as this. We ull goo down to Sauldin pond one a these nights and I ull show ye him.

Chawley   I shall taiak a good stick.'

Jim   You leave him alooan; he won't hurt ye. If ye got a-messin him about, thaiur's no telling what he ood do!

Chawley   Well good night all.

Jim   Good night. Keep your eyes open when you're gooin down. Look well into the hedge!

Chawley   Goodnight Jim. Shant believe these things you a told us about tonight.

Jim   Pleeas yurself. They be all true.

All of the above extracts are reproduced with thanks to Harman, H., *Buckinghamshire Dialect*, Hazell, Watson & Viney Ltd., London & Aylesbury, 1929.

16

The Quarrendon Centaur

M YTHICAL beasts and strange apparitions are the stuff of nightmares and horror – but what if you found yourself confronted by such a sight? 'Run like hell' might be the best advice, and that was exactly what Richard and John did in the countryside around Quarrendon near Aylesbury. Over 20 years later, they still don't want to venture back.

The story begins at the end of a lovely June day in 1988, when Richard met up with John and his German Shepherd dog, Sheba, to go for a walk across Quarrendon fields. This particular part of Quarrendon, bordered on one side by Meadowcroft Road, was very much wasteland, and only really used by dog walkers and kids playing there and in the sluggish brook with a sewage pipe running across it – known locally as the old green pipeline. Unfortunately it was also used as a dumping ground for rubbish and was not the most appealing piece of countryside, but for Sheba it was a great open space in which to run.

It was around 10.15 pm on that warm summer night. Richard and John chatted away as Sheba went on ahead, taking in the myriad of scents. Suddenly, Sheba flew back past them, running at tremendous speed. They turned and shouted after her to come back, but she did not break her stride, and did not even turn to acknowledge John's command, she just sped back the way she had come. Something had really frightened her – or was she chasing a rabbit or cat? Whatever had happened, this was totally out of character for the obedient dog they knew her to be.

They both turned back to see what might have frightened her and, yes, there was something up ahead, but what on earth was it? They gazed in fascination at a creature that clearly had the hindquarters of a horse. Its flanks were a kind of dull grey-white colour. But it was not a horse, nor any kind of livestock they recognised.

'What the hell's that?' exclaimed John.

'I don't know,' replied Richard, 'but it doesn't look like anything I've ever seen before.'

As they moved closer, the creature suddenly raised itself up and turned towards them – then the men saw that, yes, it was a type of animal, but the grey flanks moulded at the front into a human torso.

Richard told me, 'I looked and couldn't believe my eyes, neither could John. He said to me, "I'm not staying around here," and we started to run back across the wasteland.' As they went, Richard turned to look back over his shoulder and could see, now clearly visible in profile, something that was half man and half horse. It was a centaur.

In such moments logic goes out of the window. A creature of ancient Greek mythology was standing staring at the fleeing figures – however impossible that seems. Now they understood Sheba's terror. The moment itself, recalled Richard, seemed frozen, in common with many such paranormal events. There was the sound of its hooves as if it was starting to follow, yet a dream-like slow motion kicked in and the speed of their flight seemed sluggish and clumsy. Then, in an instant, it was over.

Reaching Meadowcroft Road they stopped and looked back across the field. Richards recalls, 'It was literally standing there and it was up high and it was just looking at us, and then it just moved quickly away and disappeared.'

What possible explanation could there be for such an extreme apparition? Of course, many people will claim that the men hallucinated and the whole episode was a figment of their imaginations.

Richard told me, 'As we were going back home, John turned round and said to me, "I'm not being funny, but that certainly wasn't human, and it wasn't animal but I haven't got a clue what it was. It was the two together," and I thought exactly the same.'

As they hoped, Sheba was already waiting for them at home and they both vowed that from that day on they would never go over to Quarrendon fields again. They looked so shaken that John's wife asked what had happened. They explained how Sheba has sensed something was wrong and fled, and they had both seen something over the fields that was half man and half horse. After the initial 'don't be silly' reaction Richard and John received when they recounted their experience, it was clear that both were deadly serious.

Richard confided to me, 'To this day – all these years later – I have carried it with me. I have told people about it and a few people say you're round the bend, but I know what John and I saw that night, and what we saw was definitely half animal and half human. It's like it only happened a few months ago, it's still so clear to me. What we saw that night definitely was not a horse, a cow or anything like that, what we saw that night was a centaur and it frightened me to death.'

The more I spoke with Richard, the more I became convinced it was a real event for both him and for John. My own research into this, frankly bizarre, paranormal experience revealed some unexpected results. In an article entitled *Seeing Centaurs*, Jerome Clark begins by saying, 'From time to time, if you're paying attention to such things or just happen to be in the right place at the right time, you may hear a story that is weird even by weirdness standards. Some years ago on a pleasant summer evening over a campfire in a state park in South Dakota, a ranger told me that a couple camping there had once made a very strange complaint. They reported – to all appearances, seriously – that a strange animal had come tearing into their recreational vehicle and done extensive damage before fleeing. It looked, they said, like something half human and half horse.' (J. Clark, 'Seeing Centaurs', *Fate Magazine*, August 2004.)

Clark also looked back at other such claims and did find stories of centaur sightings in rural England – unfortunately the precise location was not mentioned. Could it have been in Buckinghamshire?

Quarrendon itself has a strong sense of historical mystery and ancient adventure about it. It contains what Aylesbury Town Council calls 'Aylesbury's hidden treasure'. Here lies the lost village of Quarrendon, an official Scheduled Ancient Monument.

The rough grass fields contain the remnants of a deserted medieval settlement. There is also evidence of a 16th-century mansion that boasted magnificent formal gardens. Indeed, it is recorded that for two days in 1592 Queen Elizabeth I was a guest of Sir Henry Lee of Ditchley at what was then Quarrendon Manor. Ghostly legends suggest that Lady Lee can still be seen in the vicinity – or perhaps it is Ann Vavasor who cohabited with Sir Henry after Lady Lee died in 1584. There had been a monument to her, at first defaced for its sinful message and now disappeared within the ruins of St Peter's church in this lost village setting. It said:

Under this stone entombed lies a fair and worthy dame,
Daughter to Henry Vavasor, Ann Vavasor her name:
She living with Sir Henry Lee for love, long time did dwell;
Death could not part them, but here they rest within one cell.

Other local folklore claims this site contains Civil War earthworks and that on nearby Weedon Hill there was a battle. However, research by English Heritage has yet to discover evidence that this was the case. Local stories circulate that the sounds of battle and horses can be heard in Quarrendon fields on certain clear nights of the year, particularly in June, a month in which Buckinghamshire saw so much Civil War fighting.

So is it possible that Richard and John encountered an apparition of a dishevelled Civil War soldier slumped around the forequarters of his horse? But if indeed it was a centaur, half man and half horse, are there, or have there ever been, such creatures?

One of the most of eminent of the world's anthropologists is Paul Tacon, whose research and scientific papers are very highly regarded. In 2000 he caused a sensation when he and his colleague, Christopher Chippendale, revealed 4,000-year-old rock paintings depicting half human, half animal creatures in Arnhem Land, Australia. Their conclusions, published by Cambridge University, indicate that centaurs actually existed. The researchers were convinced that the paintings were not done from the imagination but were a record of what had been seen. Many more have now been located at Wollemi National Park in New South Wales. Tacon said, 'It is like an ancient world that time forgot. We've never seen anything quite like this combination of rare representations in so many layers.'

Did that ancient world discover a time portal in rural Buckinghamshire in the 1980s? Richard and John still have no doubts about that at all, and, it seems, nor did Sheba.

17

The Force of Truth: Aston Sandford and the Spirit of Thomas Scott

'... the soul is capable of exerting its powers and faculties, in a state of separation from the body.' (Thomas Scott, *Essays on the Most Important Subjects in Religion*, D. Jaques, London, 1880.)

S OUTH of Haddenham, in the village of Aston Sandford, lies the parish church of St Michael and All Angels. Like most ancient churches, some parts such as the nave date from the 12th century, while others such as the chancel are from a century later, with most restoration having been carried out in the late-Victorian period.

What makes this Buckinghamshire limestone church unique, however, is its size. It is one of the smallest churches in the country. It is also claimed to be the smallest haunted church in the country. The rectory is much more recent, built in the early 19th century by a remarkable rector whose ghost is now said to continue to attend evensong, standing beside the pulpit.

The Revd Thomas Scott was a strong religious force in 18th and 19th century Buckinghamshire, and clearly features in ecclesiastical historical significance alongside the legendary John Newton and William Cowper of nearby Olney, particularly in terms of spiritual awakenings and fervent evangelical commitment.

Ordained in 1772, Thomas Scott was first a curate in the parish of Stoke Goldington and then in Weston Underwood, moving on to

Ravenstone where he began a correspondence and friendship with the hymn writer John Newton. However, he did not, at this time, possess the extraordinary preaching power of Newton whose Olney church was constantly packed as villagers flooded in to hear his passionate sermons. According to Hindmarsh, 'after months of anxiety over his ineffectual pastoral ministry, and remorse over the levity with which he entered holy orders, Thomas Scott shuts himself up in his study with his Bible, the works of Richard Hooker and other Anglican divines, and by Christmas 1777 argues himself into evangelical conviction.' (D.B. Hindmarsh, 'The Olney Autobiographers', *The Journal of Ecclesiastical History*, CUP, 1998.)

The result was a new passion for spirituality and a deeply felt autobiography called *The Force of Truth: An Authentic Narrative*, published in 1779 while he was curate of Ravenstone and Weston Underwood. In this book, he revealed himself as a man 'in an awful state of mind', a man who had entered holy orders with little regard for them, actually calling himself 'a dangerous heretic'. He revealed his strong dislike for prayer on the one hand but his enjoyment of sin on the other along with a serious neglect of his parishioners. However, perhaps the following admission provided some kind of spiritual turning point: 'In January 1774, two of my parishioners, a man and his wife, lay at the point of death. I had heard of the circumstance, but according to my general custom, not being sent for, I took no notice of it; 'till one evening, the woman being now dead, and the man dying, I heard my neighbour Mr Newton had been several times to visit them. Immediately my conscience reproached me with being shamefully negligent in sitting at home within a few doors of dying persons ... and never going to visit them.'

From this experience emerged a committed, fervent preacher able to take over from Newton in Olney and then spend time with him in London founding the Church Missionary Society. When he became rector of Aston Sandford in 1803 he brought so much energy, commitment and deep evangelical passion to this small village and its tiny church, it seems it became almost impregnated with his presence and his determination never again to neglect his parishioners. During the 18 years he spent in this small Buckinghamshire village he *became* that church and when he died in 1821 he was buried beneath the altar.

Since that time he has been seen by a variety of parishioners at evensong at least a dozen times as an apparition beside the pulpit. One witness confirmed he has been visible for some minutes before gradually fading away.

Perhaps it is the case, as stated by the Revd David Horner in the story of Ellesborough (see Chapter 8), that passionate, powerful emotions – such as the burdensome guilt expressed by the Revd Thomas Scott – can create an imprint on the atmosphere around a key location that perpetuates some form of supernatural imagery after death. The rector's burial place beneath the altar no doubt has great significance and 'The Force of Truth' well and truly keeps his presence in this unique Buckinghamshire location.

Meanwhile the Revd Scott awaits your attendance at evensong.

18

The Hell-Fire Caves of West Wycombe

'Will the team find paranormal activity in the Hell-Fire Caves – the headquarters of an ancient, secret satanic society? Do the ghosts of former members still practise their evil rituals in these caves? Or, does a vengeful spirit walk through this macabre maze of tunnels? And who runs the risk of getting lost in this underground labyrinth?'

THIS dramatic television voice-over introduced a 2007 music-thumping episode of the cult American television series *TAPS* and its two ghost-hunting stars, Jason Hawes and Grant Wilson.

TAPS, or The Atlantic Paranormal Society, had discovered Buckinghamshire and in particular West Wycombe's famous tourist attraction, the Hell-Fire Caves. This place is no stranger to the media and has been the backdrop for films, advertisements and TV series such as *Inspector Morse*. Even the children's television programme *Chucklevision* has been there. In so many ways, this Buckinghamshire location seems to have been waiting for the exaggerated drama of the television ghost-hunters. The caves had already made their supernatural debut on the British television programme *Most Haunted* back in 2004 and scores of other paranormal investigators have made a pilgrimage to West Wycombe for a supernatural experience.

So, is this a genuine supernatural site with a story to tell or merely an excitingly dark and spooky collection of tunnels and caves?

The dramatic history of this place is real enough and its supernatural pedigree is so well established that we now have the luxury of several centuries of investigations to draw on. How did this rural hamlet become associated with an ancient satanic society and why should that lead to claims of supernatural activities?

It began innocently enough – or did it? Wycombe was rich in flint, which was used for building purposes, and soft chalk, easily mined and invaluable for foundations and bedding down paths and roadways. Chalk quarries were already established in the area, and this particular West Wycombe opencast quarry was well worked. Local flint had been used to build St Lawrence's church at the top of the hill, on the edge of the tiny hamlet.

However, in the late 1740s, the local rural economy was severely threatened by a series of droughts leading to poor harvests and widespread unemployment and poverty for villagers. In 1747, the 2nd Baronet, Sir Francis Dashwood, in what was a revolutionary move for that period, introduced a poor-relief bill into the House of Commons that proposed to provide employment at a fair wage by creating public work projects such as road building. This made no progress among his contemporaries, so he took it upon himself to instigate such works and pay for them out of his own pocket. 'I am determined that they shall have employment,' he said.

The wealthy Dashwood family's association with West Wycombe dated back to the 1670s and Sir Francis (1708–1781) had already overseen the building of an architectural and landscaping masterpiece on his own vast estate. Fired up by concern for his constituents, he set about organising the excavation of chalk from the opencast quarry in order to provide a new road from West Wycombe to High Wycombe. He employed around 100 men at a generous one shilling a day to mine the chalk whilst another 50 or so built the road. His flair for construction and design and his passion for the classical architecture of Athens and Rome led him to ensure that the miners fashioned the most intricate labyrinth of caves a quarter of a mile into the hillside, dipping to 300 ft beneath the church.

It is at this point that the 'other' Sir Francis Dashwood needs to be revealed. There are claims that under the cover of providing much-needed work for the local economy and being praised for his generosity and local spirit, Sir Francis harboured ulterior motives of a dark and sinister kind. Why were the caves cut in a way that replicated symbolic features deeply embedded in classical mythology and ancient Athenian cults linked to mysticism? But then aren't all wealthy aristocrats entitled to a folly or two? This one, however, was to become inextricably linked to Satanism and moral turpitude. Devil faces and demon heads are still to be found carved deep into the chalky passageways.

His creation of an underground river Styx, a symbolic boundary separating the world of the mortal from the world of the immortal, would become the touchstone of the caves' later supernatural characterisation. Across it was the Inner Temple, positioned at the farthest and deepest point of the caves directly beneath the church, conjuring up the juxtaposition of Heaven and Hades. Whilst it was never claimed that Dashwood's entrance to Hades across the river Styx was guarded by the legendary three-headed giant dog Cerberus, it soon became symbolic in its own right as direct mockery of the church above.

At the same time that Dashwood was proposing his poor-relief bill in the House, and before the caves were built, he had already created the Knights of St Francis of Wycombe. This group of eminent men would meet at Medmenham Abbey, a little over 6 miles outside Wycombe, under the motto '*Fay ce que voudras*'. Translated as 'Do as you please', it set the scene for rumours and torrid tales of drinking, womanising and devil worship. Sir Francis was head of a so-called 'Inner Circle' and revered as 'Prior of the Abbey' and there would be an annual appointment of an 'Abbot' whose main perk was first choice of the women invited to a weekend 'Chapter' meeting.

Orgies at Medmenham became more than just a rumour: '… a coterie of profane wits and politicians made a mockery of monastic rites at Medmenham to cloak their sins' (*The Times*, 29 March 1920). They soon became known as the Hell-Fire Club of England, drinking and eating to excess and womanising on a legendary scale.

An important 'player' on the scene, who would become significant in establishing the supernatural pedigree of the Hell-Fire Caves, was the poet and satirist Paul Whitehead. 'Into the circle also came Paul Whitehead as Steward of the unholy order to chalk the score of the blasphemous revellers behind the abbey door' (*The Times*, as above).

It was claimed that the 'monks' would be scored by Whitehead on their drinking ability, many consuming bottles of port and claret in vast numbers. According to Daniel P. Mannix's study (1961): 'The Hell-Fire Club: Orgies were their pleasure, Politics their pastime.' Cocktails with names such as 'Strip Me Naked', 'Lay Me down Softly' and 'Gin and Sin' were also popular. He recounts how even roast beef would be served under the name 'Devil's Loins' – expertly cut into the shape of large buttocks, served with bread called 'Holy Ghost Pye'.

So secret was the society no one knows exactly what went on but it was clear that 'wild rites' were central to the order and *The Times* claimed that: 'Satan received the crapulent homage of the pseudo-monks.'

The intricate planning and design of the caves clearly seemed to be purpose-built for Hell-Fire Club uses. There was a magnificent Gothic flint and gated entrance hall, leading down a long passage, past small, intimate chambers or cells to a wondrous banqueting hall 50 ft high and 40 ft in diameter. The Club's famous Rosicrucian crystal lamp with its entwined serpent of pure gold symbolising eternity hung from the centre of the ceiling, throwing a mystical glow over the cavorting and feasting.

From here runs a clever triangular path system, said to have a sexual symbolism, past another cave, now known as the miners' cave, to the river Styx. Here was dug a 'cursing well' filled with 'unholy water' to 'baptise' new members to this exclusive Satanist club. Beyond this symbolic river, crossed by boat, lay the Hell-Fire Club's Inner Temple 300 ft below St Lawrence's church. Here, it is claimed, black masses would be held which required young girls to sacrifice their virginity to selected members of the Club. The small cells en route to the banqueting hall and beyond were used for similar purposes but, more often than not, with prostitutes dressed as nuns – so called dollymops – in the orgiastic build-up to the ultimate black mass event and sacrifice of the innocents directly beneath the holy church on the hill above, mocking Christianity both symbolically and in reality.

Philanthropist and Satanist? Sir Francis was a complex man who clearly assisted his local villagers who desperately needed work, but gained a private underground headquarters for his Hell-Fire Club. At the same time, he was also having the church of St Lawrence rebuilt as it was in a state of serious disrepair. The restored church was crowned by a huge golden ball in which Sir Francis was able to sit with up to half a dozen other friends and drink 'divine punch' gazing from 'heaven' across the Buckinghamshire countryside.

He had managed to do what no other man had ever done. He had designed and built his own heaven and hell, one directly above the other as it was meant to be. But why is the hell side of his creation credited with supernatural significance in the 21st century rather than being viewed as a mere folly?

Before we enter the Hell-Fire Caves with Jason Hawes and Grant Wilson's *TAPS* team and all the other paranormal investigators and tourists to find out, we need to recount two crucial events relating to two significant people. One is Paul Whitehead, to whom we have been introduced (albeit briefly), the other is a young village girl called Sukie (a derivation of Susan).

We have seen that Paul Whitehead became the Steward of the Hell-Fire Club, responsible for the Cellar Book, in which he detailed the members' consumption of alcohol for later settlement, and for keeping other records of the Club's activities – these, it was claimed, he burnt in the days just before his death. He was Sir Francis Dashwood's devoted friend, and they shared secrets about the Hell-Fire Club that both took to their respective graves. When Paul Whitehead died in 1774, he literally left his heart to Sir Francis, with money to pay for the ancient rite of a heart-burial. Leaving his body to medical science, he bequeathed £50 of his estate to be spent on a marble urn in which his heart should be laid and which Sir Francis should place in his family mausoleum 'as a memorial of its warm attachment to the noble Founder'. A solemn funeral was held for Whitehead's heart as the urn was carried three times around the mausoleum by soldiers of the Bucks Militia, while the St Lawrence church choir sang a hymn that had been specially composed for the occasion.

It was in 1781 that the first supernatural events began, which have continued until this day. Household staff at West Wycombe Park, home to an increasing frail Sir Francis, were scared witless on seeing the ghost of Paul Whitehead in the grounds looking towards Sir Francis and beckoning him to join him. Betty Puttick, in *Ghosts of Buckinghamshire* (1995), quotes Lady Austin, Dashwood's sister, writing to a friend about this haunting: 'There are few, if any, of his lordship's numerous household who have not likewise seen him (the ghost) sometimes in the Park, sometimes in the garden, as well as in the house by day and night.'

In December of that same year, Sir Francis joined his loyal steward in death.

There it might have all ended – but in 1839, in a macabre incident, someone stole Paul Whitehead's heart from the urn as a souvenir. After the Hell-Fire Caves were opened to the public in the 1950s, it is said that many reports have been made by visitors seeing a man resembling Paul Whitehouse searching for his heart both in the mausoleum and down in the caves.

But there is another supernatural episode to add to our journey into the caves, which also links us to the nearby village inn, the George and Dragon. Unproven, but still rumoured, is the claim that this ancient hostelry has a secret connecting tunnel to the hillside caves. Whilst the alcoholic and sexual excesses associated with the Hell-Fire Club formed the main gossip here in the early 18th century, a young girl called Sukie was working at the tavern. Local lads were keen rivals for her affection but she wanted more than they could offer. Before long, an aristocratic gentleman was smitten by her beauty and became a regular visitor to the inn. Whether he had any connections with the Hell-Fire Club is not clear, but Sukie saw him as her means of escaping her lowly status and becoming a lady. Excited, she received a letter one day, seemingly from her wealthy admirer, professing his love for her and his desire for her to run away with him that very night. He asked her to wear her best white dress as a bridal gown and meet with him in the caves.

Whether she knew of a secret tunnel or went across the village street and along to the cave entrance is not known, but using a flame torch, she arrived in the caves, dressed in her white finery, eagerly looking for her suitor. When three village lads appeared and no young aristocrat, Sukie realised she was the victim of a cruel hoax. In temper she picked up a lump of chalk and flung it at the boys, one of whom retaliated – she fell badly and lay still. The story has two endings, neither of which can be proved to be the correct version. In one, the three lads ran off to summon help and she was taken back to her room at the George and Dragon where she died, despite a local doctor's best attempts to save her. In the other, she was left to die in the caves before being found and taken back to the inn.

Since her death, many people have reported seeing the ghost of a distressed young woman, all in white, both in the George and Dragon and in the Hell-Fire Caves. Many had absolutely no knowledge of the original tragedy – they were often overseas visitors who were taken completely by surprise at what they had seen and then amazed once they learned about poor Sukie's tragic demise.

One traveller staying at the George and Dragon in 1966 was a well-known American freelance writer called Jhan Robbins. He pointed out to the waiting staff that his treacle pudding had a hole in it, as if someone's thumb had been pushed into it. They apologised and explained it was typical of Sukie's presence in the tavern. This was one of her tricks to show she was about. Fascinated by Sukie's story, he asked if he could stay in her old room that night.

During the night he experienced an icy cold hand pressed to his forehead, not once but several times. In the dark room, he watched as a small pinpoint of light grew bigger and bigger, reaching about 4 ft high and 2 ft wide, having, as he described, an 'opaque, pearly quality'. Scared but determined, he walked towards it into the most intense cold he had ever experienced. His limbs became leaden, his breathing laboured, and he was overwhelmed by feelings of sadness and depression. As the shape pushed forward to engulf him, he panicked, turned and put on the light. There was nothing there. A dream perhaps after a good meal? He emphatically denied it. He was convinced he had seen Sukie's ghost.

Right up to the present time, there have been many attempts to collect supernatural 'evidence' in the caves. A UK organisation called Paranormal Tours has made at least half a dozen investigative studies using clairvoyant mediums, paranormal enthusiasts and, assisted by Hell-Fire Caves employees, has attempted to discover what is going on in those dark tunnels. They recount the story of a mother taking her two children into the caves. The family thoroughly enjoyed the expedition and came back to the coffee shop for refreshments. The mother was interested to know who was having the wedding in the caves that day, commenting on how unusual it was to have such a facility. The bemused Hell-Fire Caves assistant said there was no such function or any facility for weddings in the caves.

The mother explained that she and her children had just seen a lady in a white wedding dress walking in the tunnel ahead of them down in the caves. The startled assistant then told her about Sukie.

Many tourists leave the caves having either sensed someone brushing past them or feeling a light touch on their heads and perhaps hearing a 'pssst' or a growl or possibly a woman's distress. In some cases they have followed a 'quaintly-dressed' distant figure, merely to see them vanish at a dead-end. Every paranormal investigation in recent years has confirmed that something is definitely going on down in the caves that defies natural explanation.

When TAPS undertook their investigation in 2007, they had access to the latest digital camera technology and highly sensitive audio equipment. They soon realised that certain noises in the dark depths of the tunnels were not supernatural at all, as many casual visitors had claimed. The chalky gravel gets kicked up by shoes, making a sound like ghostly footsteps. The random dripping of water from the ceiling and crevices also makes strange echoes, often dripping onto people who think they have been touched on the head. Slight draughts from small cave-cells brush lightly past and temperature changes occur. These are all natural phenomena.

But when they played back their audio files from machines left in the depths of the notorious Inner Temple, there, without doubt, were the sounds of a growling voice and then another terse male voice, the words very indistinct but they were words nonetheless.

In the area where a young woman in a white dress has been reported by visitors and investigators over the centuries, the audio evidence revealed a female voice attempting a sentence, her indistinct speech interlaced with that of the investigators, whose conversations at the time were also being recorded. They were totally unaware of this additional voice until they played back their recordings.

But for Jason Hawes and Grant Wilson, their own 'highly experienced neck hairs' were pricked when they viewed what had been captured by a camera facing a dead end by the Inner Temple. Absolutely no one from the TAPS team was in the tunnel at the time – there was just a camera set to record whatever came towards it. A light begins to show, then increases as if 'someone' is moving nearer. The illumination is such that the sides of the chalk tunnels are lit with a strange florescent glow.

It is unlike any flashlight, more akin to a flame-torch coming closer, but there is no flicker of flame. Whitehead? Sukie? Another resident spirit? Whatever it was it did not reveal itself in human form.

When this was shown to Hell-Fire Caves employee Teresa Tedman, the unexplained image became even more significant. She confided to the team, for the first time, that she had personally experienced the same phenomenon but thought she might have been imagining things.

'Wow, you didn't tell us!' exclaimed Grant. 'And nobody was down there?' questioned Jason.

'Nobody, I was the only one,' confirmed Teresa. 'I was down by the Inner Temple, I looked up the tunnel and there was a light on the wall where I knew one of our lights wasn't and I stood back and looked and as I walked up the tunnel, it disappeared.'

Teresa seemed very relieved that what she thought had been her imagination had now been caught on camera by a team of professional investigators: '... you don't know how far your imagination stretches when you are by yourself down the caves, so for somebody else to have that experience – it validated what I saw.'

All kinds of people continue to be touched by the supernatural in West Wycombe's Hell-Fire Caves, whether it is a man wandering in search of his heart, or a young woman in white, distressed and angry. Also there is another powerful personality that other investigators say they have sensed in the caves – an American one, and it's not Jason or Grant.

Benjamin Franklin, a close friend of Sir Francis, visited on several occasions and even wrote to an American colleague, 'His Lordship's imagery, puzzling and whimsical as it may seem, is as much evident below the earth as it is above it.'

But is it much more than this? Are the Hell-Fire Caves a site of on-going supernatural activity below the earth – in a man-made hell? It seems that they just might well be. Let Jason Hawes, founder of TAPS, have the last word: 'I believe the place is haunted.'

Endispiece

B UCKINGHAMSHIRE ghosts have flitted past us in a variety of guises during the telling of these stories, whether in human form, misty orb-like shapes, sounds, smells, or just a 'feeling' – something glimpsed – but then nothing is there.

I started the research for this book not as a newcomer to supernatural happenings, I have covered such areas before – but I did question and dig and prod at all the accounts that came my way for ordinary, everyday explanations rather than other-worldly ones.

I am convinced that we are poised on so many boundaries and explanations other than mere commonsense ones. Whether that boundary is a ley line, pulsing with energy, an astral plane, a time-slip, a spiritual portal, a trapped soul living yet dead – the supernatural is there to explore.

Before we leave them all behind, I would like to add one final story – an old 'scrap' of Buckinghamshire supernatural folklore.

Around 1910, Mrs Cadle from Long Crendon, a famous needle-making hamlet in Buckinghamshire, told a story to author Geoffrey Gomme who was collecting what he termed 'scraps of English folklore'. The story was one told to her by her grandmother and concerns two elderly women living together in a Long Crendon farmhouse, long ago demolished and replaced by a house known as the Mound.

One of the women had been married, the other was a spinster. The elderly widow lay dying and, in a terrible act of theft, her spinster companion stole her wedding ring from her finger. The widow vowed that as soon as she died, she'd haunt her treacherous friend for this despicable deed. Indeed, after the widow's death, the spinster had to endure constant feelings of pin-pricks to her body that grew worse if she ventured to relax under the shade of the garden's magnificent elm tree.

So intense was the haunting persecution that she arranged to 'capture' the ghost of her tormentor in a salt box that was kept by the fire to keep its contents dry. According to Geoffrey Gomme, twelve parsons came to the house and in unison chanted a prayer backwards, whilst one parson held aloft a dove of peace. He recounts, 'The spirit, in the shape of the woman, tore the dove into pieces and then went into the salt box there to remain "whilst water runs and the sun shines".'

I finish as I began – dealing with the supernatural, on occasions, does benefit from 'a good pinch of salt'

Bibliography

Harman, H., *Buckinghamshire Dialect*, Hazell, Watson & Viney, 1929
Hicks, C., *The Green Man*, Compass Books, 2000
Kidd-Hewitt, D., *Buckinghamshire Tales of Mystery & Murder*, Countryside Books, 2003
Kitchener, L., *The Heart and Soul of Olney*, Lewis Kitchener, 2004
Mack L., et al. eds, *The World of the Unexplained*, Orbis 1984,
Mannix, D.P., *The Hell-Fire Club*, New English Library, 1967
Pilgrim, J., *"Out and About"* with John Pilgrim, Alpine Press Ltd, 1999
Phillips, D., '*The Green Man of Fingest*' in Cleaver, A., Strange Wycombe, Thame House, 1991
Rae-Ellis, V., *True Ghost Stories of our own time*, Faber & Faber, 1990
Ratcliff, O., *Olney, Bucks*, Cowper Press , Olney 1907
Rice, H.S., *Ghosts of the Chilterns and Thames Valley*, Corinthian Publishers, 1983
Scott, T., *The Force of Truth: an authentic narrative*, R. Carter, 1798
TAPS: Hell-fire Caves Episode 42: Season 3: 2007
Alison Uttley, *Buckinghamshire*, Robert Hale, 1950

ARTICLES
Barber, R., *Interview with Cilla Black* in the Daily Mail *Weekend Magazine*, 19th January 2008
Clark, J., '*Seeing Centaurs*'. Fate Magazine, August 2004.
Gomme, G.I.L., et.al., '*Scraps of English Folklore*' Folklore, Vol.21. No 2. June 1910
Hindmarsh, D., B., '*The Olney Autobiographers: English Conversion Narrative in the Mid-Eighteenth Century,*' The Journal of Ecclesiastical History (1998), 49: CUP
Raglan, Lady., '*The "Green Man" in Church Architecture*' Folklore Vol.50, No 1 March 1939
Swann, J., '*Shoes Concealed in Buildings*', in Costume, No. 30, 1996, pp.56-69 (Journal of the Costume Society: Dorset)

NEWSPAPERS
The Bucks Free Press; The Bucks Herald; The Milton Keynes Citizen; South Bucks Free Press; South Bucks Star; The Times

Index